LIFE ON YOUR TERMS

CREATE THE LIFE YOU WANT

REX STEVEN SIKES

LAID-BACK BUDDHA PRESS

Edited by Tony Petrozza & Tim Shay
Cover Design by Dan Brezgel
Book design and production by IDEA Seminars & Rex Sikes Entertainment, LLC

PRAISE FOR LIFE ON YOUR TERMS

"This book is loaded with powerful insights and ideas that motivate and inspire you to accomplish great things. Get ready to change your life in a wonderful way." – Brian Tracy Author 'Maximum Achievement'

"Eye-opening! Answers questions everyone has had about how to REALLY live the life of their dreams! Empowering! Read it!" – Dr. Joe Vitale Author of "The Miracle," Star of The Secret

"Rex Sikes' book Life On Your Terms is brilliant! It offers cutting-edge tools that take you to another level. It's a practical manual with a fresh take on personal growth and transformation that's infused with love, wisdom, and some truly innovative ideas. I am reading it daily and it's changing my life. Not only do I feel a shift in consciousness but I have been waking up happier. This book offers hope to anyone who has lost their way in life." – Lydia Cornell Actor 'Too Close For Comfort

"Rex Sikes is a walking inspiration. He inspires the inspirers, which is why I love the way he thinks, lives, and teaches. In this book, he deconstructs the myths of the law of attraction and makes it easier to understand how to apply it to your everyday thought process. It's one thing to wish and want something, and another to apply these laws effectively, which really do work. Why do some people appear to have everything and end up having nothing, while others have the true inner-secret to love, success, (whatever that means to you) and inner peace? Joy is there to be ours, peace is there to be ours, blessings are there to be ours, it is all about focus and harnessing our thoughts, dreams, and desires by using Rex Sikes simple and effective techniques. You must understand to apply, let Rex be your guide and your life can change no matter what you've been through." – Catherine Hickland Actor 'One Life To Live', Author, Hypnotist

"Rex is absolutely brilliant and transparent. My go-to book for those I mentor who want to be happy and successful with their lives as they choose." – Fred Van Lieu 'The Water Doctor,' Author

"Yes, you can achieve anything, and Rex tells you how to do it. He gives you pages of real-life principles shown to change lives. These can absolutely work for you. All you have to do is live these principles and you become the winner." – Pete Bissonette, Author, Learning Strategies Corporation

"Rex's background as change agent, actor, magician, mentalist, communicator, performer, and survivor, makes him well practiced in the art of knowing the inner landscape of the human mind. In this book, he hands you the keys to unlock the magical kingdom within you. Not only do you receive the keys, codes, and passwords, you also get the full behind-the-scenes tour to know how to use them. You can now take charge of your own thinking and enjoy the abundant riches you are uniquely qualified to produce as you live life on your own terms." – Paul R. Scheele, Ph.D., CEO, Scheele Learning Systems and co-founder of Learning Strategies Corporation

"Rex Sikes has taken many of life's most relevant topics for success, and expressed them in a way that each of us are able to relate, value and apply to our lives. It's easy to journey through life and get into routines that leave us passing time with no improvement or excellence to celebrate. Rex offers practical methods, built on the basic platform of human psychology and inner development for anyone to comprehend. Overcoming personal barriers and navigating our way around life's roadblocks, is what determines our quality of life. You will find the juicy nuggets expressed in this book, to help you do just that. Now sit back, and turn the pages as you begin a little journey of personal discovery!" – Scott Fardulis, Network Marketing Professional

"As one of the 'Top 25 Network Marketers in World' and also a recovering alcoholic with over 30 years sobriety, I am constantly asked to review and read books on personal development either in business or recovery. Most of them are just like the last one I read. Nothing ever seems new or too useful.

And then came Life On Your Terms by Rex Sikes. From the first page, I knew this book would be different and better. And the more I read the more right I was. This book has been haunting me in almost every area of my life. I am now controlling my thoughts instead of just being with them.

Sikes was "one of us." Just stuck in the muck. And like me, he had to change literally everything in his life. But he decided to start his change between his ears. And the book details that to the max. He showed me how to "move the furniture around in my head". And learn to make the most of every minute in every day. He made me realize that change for me literally started with my first thought of the day. I was almost instantly happier.

As I read on the book just took me deeper and deeper into what is absolutely possible for me in my life with literally no help from anyone else. But on the flip side of that, he showed me why I so need people around me.

Read this book. It will change your life. Even if your life is great, like mine is today, it will make it even better. I have so many people reading it, from my son to my AA friends to my business associates, because it works for everyone. I LOVE THIS BOOK!" – Tom Chenault, The Tom Chenault Radio Show & co-founder of ContactMapping.com

"Having seen an early version Life On Your Terms, I can say it has the potential to be life-changing, and help many people. Much of the self-help leaders focus on trying to differentiate and distinguish themselves in crowded marketplace. They're always trying to teach that one secret that nobody else provides. Sure, it is sexy for marketing and often useful. Yet, people lose sight of the 20% action practices that delivers 80% of the results. They forget the concept of true mastery of this 20%. There is great power within the 20%. I appreciate how your 80% is that powerful 20%. You then add in other stuff to fill in people's blind-spots, expand awareness, and take people to the next level.

You are focusing 80% on the 20% that delivers 80 % of the results! Most of the self-improvement, NLP, and LOA world seem to focus on the low impact stuff, to the point where many people don't even recognize or appreciate the 20% that delivers 80% of the results. 80% of those who do recognize the essential 20% aren't taking habitual action and achieving mastery of the 20%. Those who master that 20% experience a shift in their world, and enjoy amazing results." – Michael Halbfish, Attorney

Free Gift Link & Product Links

Click Link To Get Free: 22 Minute Downloadable Mp3
'Your Biggest Problem And What To Do About It' Audio gift. In 22 Minutes You Will Discover What Is Holding You Back From Success! Stop Struggling. End Negativity. Learn How To Develop A Powerful Mindset And Live The Life You Deserve. Get Your Free Gift Today! (A $29 value!)

https://ideaseminars.mykajabi.com/WHATS-STOPPING-YOU-GIFT

A Powerful Tool To Assist You In Creating The Life You Deserve And Great Accompaniment To This Book And Home Study Program

https://ideaseminars.mykajabi.com/attitude-activator-special-offer

Click Link To Purchase: Change Your Thoughts And Transform Your Life: Law Of Attraction Home Study Program

The Home Study Program - Includes audio, video and comprehensive workbook. Explode your ability to manifest and create your best life ever using this powerful and practical course. Work at your own pace.

https://ideaseminars.mykajabi.com/changeyourthoughtsLOA

Visit IDEA Seminars at idea-seminars.com

Disclaimer

The material in this book is not intended to be psychological, medical, financial, or legal advice. Seek the appropriate counsel for those and other needs. The author is not liable for use or misuse of the information presented.

Although the author and publisher have made every effort to ensure that the information in this book was correct at press time, the author and publisher do not assume and hereby disclaim any liability to any party for any loss, damage, or disruption caused by errors or omissions, whether such errors or omissions result from negligence, accident, or any other cause.

This book is not intended as a substitute for the medical advice of physicians. The reader should regularly consult a physician in matters relating to his/her health and particularly with respect to any symptoms that may require diagnosis or medical attention. The information in this book is not meant to replace proper treatment.

Thank god I never became a lawyer…that might have been rough for many of us. But keep that in mind as you read this. And that's it for my CYA statement.

So, let's begin!

Acknowledgements

People I deeply appreciate and want to thank:

Tony Petrozza and Tim Shay for editing the manuscript. Tony is very dedicated to doing the best and I benefited greatly from his efforts and enthusiasm. Michael Halbfish for reviewing the manuscript numerous times. Dan Brezgel for cover design. Tim Shay for editing, making links work and a whole host of other things. For being a true talent and incredibly knowledgeable. Tim really helped get things done. Kim Van Meter for tirelessly working to format and ready kindle and book for publication. This would not have been possible without her.

The wonderful people who contributed their stories, anonymously and otherwise. So many heroes.

The wonderful people who read the book and have said many kind things about it and about me. Karen Barben, Pete Bissonette, Scott Fardulis, Tom Chenault, Lydia Cornell, Catherine Hickland, Paul Scheele, Brian Tracy, Fred Van Lieu, Joe Vitale. Each of these incredible people is a champion in their own right and have created marvelous lives for themselves. I am honored and privileged to know them.

My mentors, and people, who have encouraged and nurtured me along the way. Sometimes they helped by challenging me and some-times by being easy on me.

My students come from around the world, in all walks of life, all colors, creeds and nationalities. I have been fortunate and enriched by knowing each of you. You contribute to me and I learn from each of you.

The great thought leaders from ancient to modern times whose wisdom and practices I have benefited from in innumerable ways. I absolutely stand on their shoulders and enjoy the ride they give me.

Everyone I have met, loved, hated, had fun with or fought because through our experiences together I have learned and evolved. Source has provided everything I have needed on this journey.

My secret brotherhood. My Sannyasi family.

My family. My children are my deepest joy and I am so blessed with the gift of them in my life.

My daughter Sydney and my son Jordan have always been a source of inspiration and motivation for living well, loving and making dreams come true. I am a lucky dad.

My sister, Gini Sikes, an author, editor, journalist, producer and Emmy Nominated filmmaker for her support, her reviews, and feedback. I am a lucky brother, too.

All named, and unnamed people, for your help, encouragement and support. You are beautiful and you are loved. Anyone I have forgotten to mention.

To you who read this book and transform your lives. Carry the torch. Help others transform too. Make a difference in the world. Spread love and peace while you create your best life and make your dreams come true.

Much love and Namaste'

CONTENTS

FOREWORD

A colleague once said to me: "The hardest thing to do is THINK". Of course, when I heard him say that, I thought to myself "You can't be serious"... but the more that I pondered that statement, the more that I grew to understand it to be relevant. As human beings in today's hectic and uber-busy world, we oftentimes resort to getting through our day on autopilot, and by default we rely on our lifetime accumulated stash of comfortable habits, just to get by without using up our perceived reserves of mental fuel. That is natural, comfortable behavior, but that doesn't always propel us enough to lift off efficiently, and take some simple steps on our own... steps that are needed for constant improvement and deserved happiness. Sometimes we all need just a little boost.

Making positive changes and tweaks in our lives, even when just revising our thought habits one small step at a time, actually does work. Rex Sikes is a living, breathing example of that. I am a living, breathing example of that. There are many other living, breathing examples of that, too, but for every one that is, there are numerous others that are not. Those that are not could certainly benefit from the lessons passed on by those that are walking, talking, living, breathing examples of "I've made these revisions to my thinking habits, and they WORK!" IT works!! As my Great-Grandfather Napoleon Hill taught: The habit of THINKING, backed by ACTION, works!! He was right.

Rex Sikes is my own present day "personal thought trainer". He provides appropriate reminders and encouragement in this book, with relevant examples that can apply to everyone - no matter their circumstance; ALL of what he writes provides daily nourishment to help sustain me personally as I plow through each day, and I am confident that it will you, too. I take delight in all of his writings, and have 're-gifted' forward many of them; to family, friends, and colleagues of mine, that continue to report back with stories of how something he has written actually influenced and recalculated the axis of their life's rotation.

So get ready to let the "thoughts" begin. Read, absorb, and enjoy!

Karen McHugh Barben

Great Granddaughter of Napoleon Hill

MY STORY

Today, I live the life of my dreams. For four decades, I've been able to do what I want, go where I want, with whom I want. I work when I want. I raised my children as a single dad, able to spend all the time I wished with them as they grew up. I've studied with the mentors I admire and travelled extensively. I am free and blessed in so many ways. Life is on my terms!

It certainly wasn't always like this. At 25 my career as an actor took a downturn. After some early successes, I was floundering. I had a wonderful girlfriend whom I wanted to marry, but could barely make ends meet. Then during a skydiving adventure (back in the days before they required that you jump tandem with an instructor I took a three-hour lesson and leapt out solo), I suffered a serious accident. Tormented from pain and unable to sleep, I sought relief from a well-credentialed medical professional.

He prescribed a combination of pills, giving me sample packets. Before leaving his Beverly Hills office to pick up my sister, I asked, "Can I take these now?"

"Sure," he replied.

That is practically all I remember from the next 18 months. Later my sister told me when I picked her up that day, I drove erratically all over the road, swearing at other drivers. On the doctor's pills, I became me so agitated that friends worried I was cracking up. Many started avoiding me. Others, trying to calm me down, shared their own medications, including Valium, Darvon, and Quaaludes. My girlfriend could see something was drastically wrong but didn't know what. I'd hid the fact I'd been injured and placed on medication for fear she'd be mad at me for skydiving. Finally she broke up with me.

Only I didn't remember that she broke up with me. I hounded her, not understanding why she refused to meet. Meanwhile I collapsed outside her or my apartment numerous times. At other times I slept in the street or park.

My parents were traveling when my sister called them to say, "Come to LA *now*. Something is horribly wrong with Rex." They arrived to find me nearly comatose, surrounded by empty pill containers, alcohol bottles, and dirty dishes. Most disturbing were the stacks of journals, volume upon volume, none containing a single sentence you could read. All filled with gibberish.

My parents locked me in my apartment, removed any last medications, took the distributor cap off my car, and hoped for the best while they deliberated checking me into a psychiatric hospital.

I went into withdrawal cold turkey. Sweating, terrified, with no clear memory of anything, I decided to end things. In a moment of despair, I screamed and ran toward my open bay window.

I plummeted two stories, crashing through the top of a tree with my neighbor's cat sitting in its branches. I landed on my head and toppled over on the grass. "Well, that didn't work," I thought. "And I killed the cat." I staggered around to the front of the building and up the stairs to my apartment to try again.

My door remained locked. Standing on the front yard, my family had missed my ridiculous nosedive and couldn't figure out how I'd escaped the locked room or what I meant by repeatedly yelling, "I killed Wendy's cat!" Actually, the cat was fine. I was not.

I collapsed on the ground and sobbed. "I don't know what's going on."

My parents took me to several psychiatrists, who marveled I was still walking. The Beverly Hills doctor had given me a dangerous combination of pills, and the other shrinks thought it a miracle I didn't die. At the very least I should have ended up in a coma. To treat me, they wanted to prescribe more drugs.

I refused. Last thing I wanted was another pill robbing me of my life. I tried various talk and alternative therapies without success. My career was now gone. My friends didn't trust me. My girlfriend and her family still shunned me.

I began to drink heavily, getting smashed daily. Then one night while inebriated in a club, an angry stranger approached me and shoved me hard in the chest. He signaled the maître d', Benson, demanding I be kicked out. I had no idea why he was livid, but somehow managed to piece together that the evening before I'd bothered him and his girlfriend. The maître d' Benson who knew me from better days, smoothed things over, explaining that I was really a good guy, I just wasn't in my own head.

After Benson saved me, I went downstairs where I found a waiter friend of mine and asked about the hothead upstairs. "I guess I was messing with him last night," I said. My friend turned pale and almost dropped his tray.

"Are you out of your mind?" he hissed. He pressed his face close to mine. "That guy is one of the most dangerous Mafia guys around. You are a disaster! You pass out in the yard, you almost drive off a cliff, and you piss off the wrong people. He will freakin' kill you. Do you *want* to die?"

I didn't. Although I'd wanted to die many times, in that moment, even blotto and confused, I knew I wanted to live.

That night I went home and reflected. Everything was wrong. I carried tremendous guilt. I felt so bad and so ashamed. I had to do something.

Since I was 11 years old, I'd practiced hypnosis and read books by Napoleon Hill, Ernest Holmes, Joseph Murphy, Norman Vincent Peale, Khalil Gibran, Eastern mystics and similar writers. I had done affirmations and meditated. But now several years had passed since I practiced. I needed to start again. I had to find a way to become calm and reclaim my life without whining, blaming, or making excuses.

I vowed to stay in my apartment and sit in my chair in a reflective state of mind and repeat affirmations until I restored myself. All day and night I affirmed and visualized while in that chair. I got up to use the bathroom and eat, but afterward, I went right back to the chair.

For more than six weeks days I sat in that chair. It was during this time that I learned the secret to turning my life around. I figured out why affirmations don't work for many people, and how to make them work powerfully for myself. I discovered how to overcome fears and limiting thoughts. While it took time, I came back bigger and better than ever. I transformed from someone who had nearly died, to being able to handle large amounts of difficulty with relative ease. I learned how to be grateful for disaster and get through it. I began to love and savor my life.

That period of 42 days was the best investment I could have ever made because it was a commitment I made to me. Now, you can use my experience to change yourself.

Does this mean you have to sit in a chair like I did for 42 days? No! I learned the hard way, but you don't have to. You can begin to transform your life by doing some simple things that will bring you exponential results. In this book I'll share with you how I acquired the ability to control my thoughts. This ability is crucial to living successfully. I learned the power of making a decision and seeing it through. I experienced the incredible strength that commitment brings. I learned to stop whining and to start winning.

After I recovered from my ordeal, I started teaching what I'd learned. I called one aspect of it Directed Questions™. I combined my personal discoveries with Neuro-Linguistic Programming (NLP), meditation, whole-brain learning, hypnosis, and other relevant disciplines. I developed a program called Mind Design™. I haven't shared the Mind Design™ method in its entirety outside of my workshops until recently. This program is one of the very special things that set my training apart from all of the others.

In these pages I share with you important thoughts, principles, and practices I teach in online programs and live events that you can use to revolutionize your life and transform yourself. Benefit from my experience. I cleared the path so you don't have to do that legwork BUT you still have to walk the path.

Imagine, if you apply these principles I share with you, what life might look like for you five years from now, three years, one year, or even 90 days? Do you want to make more money, have more fun, and enjoy more free time for family and friends? Is your life worth it? If you answer, "yes" then do it!

There's a lot more to my story, but this is enough for now. Join me in making your dreams come true!

Start living your life on your own terms!

"Attitude is a choice. Happiness is a choice. Optimism is a choice. Kindness is a choice. Giving is a choice. Respect is a choice. Whatever choice you make makes you. Choose wisely." — Roy T. Bennett,

PRELUDE

UNLESS YOU DO THIS YOU ARE BOUND TO FAIL

For nearly 40 years I have asked this question in articles, presentations and seminars near and far, 'What is it that stops most people?' What is it that prevents people from being happy, having the career they want, a great relationship and living their dreams?

Some answer 'fear.' Some say 'doubt.' Others answer 'procrastination,' or 'apathy.' Others chime in 'struggle,' 'it's too hard.' Failure. They give up. I get many similar answers. What is the bottom line? What are all of these made of? What is common to each of these answers?

Each answer is a thought. It may be spoken or silent, but it is a thought. A mental packet of electrochemical energy, is what stops most people. People think they are afraid. They have thoughts of doubt. They think it is too hard. They've tried and are convinced they can't succeed. They think, 'I'll do it later.' These thoughts are beliefs people use to justify inaction and helplessness. They're not real.

Who You Think You Are Or Are Not Can Hold You Back

They're thoughts. This is precisely why I have been a champion for gaining control of what goes on in your head, between your ears, and in your body for decades. People allow themselves to lose out, miss out, not have what they want and don't even try, because of what they repeatedly think day in and day out.

The truth is this! All it is, is a habit. You think it otherwise? Of course, you do and that is the point. People have learned lines of thinking they repeat blindly throughout the years that determine the course of their lives, and they do not change it. They entertain electro-chemical packets of energy and let that stop them.

These are thought habits. They think the same thing over and over and wonder why life doesn't change. It won't either, unless people change what they learned to do so well. They need to change their thought habits. In order to change, one needs to know a change is necessary. One needs to become aware. One needs awareness!

Discipline Is Your Friend Not Your Enemy - Create Good Habits

Then, one needs to know what to change, and actually change it. If you are engaged in a non-supportive or destructive habit then you must first realize it is the habit causing the problems and replace the habit with a better, supportive, productive one. Get it? You must do something. You can't do nothing and expect changes

If you do nothing, everything remains the same. Some people try many things; they change jobs, they try to diet, they change partners, they move to different locations but their thinking remains the same. That is why they date or marry the same person again and again. That is why they end up in debt again and again.

That is why they find themselves repeating the same mistakes in different places. Their thinking remained the same. Take charge of your thinking and you can begin to change everything for the better. You can improve your life. You can improve everything, but nothing will change, unless YOU change!

The Only Difference Between A Good And Bad Day Is Attitude

After all, it is only a thought. Thoughts can be changed. The thoughts you think are the basis for your feelings and your actions. What you think and believe creates your reality, your present and your tomorrow. Your thoughts form your experiences. Beliefs can be defined as habitual thoughts you repeatedly think.

Learn to change your thoughts! Learn to manage your thoughts. Learn to take charge of your thinking and you will improve your life! Everything can begin to change when you choose what you think.

You win, when you tell your brain what to think, instead of your brain telling you. Take charge! Stop being a victim of your thinking and become a victor. Put your brain to work for you. Choose and live life on your terms. Take what you read here and apply it! The principles and practices you learn from my experience will help you find the power within you to create your best life ever. Celebrate everything!

"Shoot for the moon, even if you miss, you'll land among the stars."
— *Les Brown*

"It's not what you say out of your mouth that determines your life, it's what you whisper to yourself that has the most power!" — *Robert Kiyosaki*

"In the process of letting go you will lose many things from the past, but you will find yourself." — *Deepak Chopra*

"You can, you should, and if you're brave enough to start, you will."
— *Stephen King*

COURSEWORK

The material I'm sharing with you in these pages comes from my online courses and live events. To date I've lead workshops and shared this material with countless numbers of people nearly 40 years. It is comprised of ancient principles, practices and the latest cutting-edge research. Apply what you learn in these pages and the world can be your oyster.

How does the brain, your subconscious, actually work? Once you understand how and why it functions, as it does, you will be able to easily work with it. You'll be able to make changes and accomplish your goals and dreams more easily. The key is to program it the same way it was originally programmed.

The reason most people don't get what they want is that they do not know how to program and work with their own brains. The fault is not theirs. Most of us are never taught how. Instead, we live life haphazardly, unless, we are fortunate enough to come across a mentor or source that can help us transform.

The brain is a servo-mechanism*. What is that? It's a servant. It works reliably and automatically. It does whatever it is programmed to do without judgment or question. It never says 'no.' It can only say, 'yes.' It doesn't even understand the concept of 'no'. That is why we can say, 'don't think of a blue elephant.'

(Maxwell Maltz may have coined the term 'servo-mechanism in Psycho-Cybernetics. I love it.)

Too late! You already did. It does not understand negation. For example, if you say, 'I am stupid', your brain says, 'yes you are'. It will find multiple examples of how this might be true for you. If you say, 'I am not stupid,' your brain drops the negation and what you are left with is 'I am stupid.' Get it? Consider this. What is the most memorable word in the sentence? If you said 'stupid,' you are definitely not.

The brain is designed for one purpose. It keeps you alive. Your survival is the primary motive. For it to succeed at this it operates in a reliable fashion. I'll get back to this in a moment but first let's discuss the subconscious. It is a system of processes.

It is not a computer; it is far more sophisticated. We can borrow some of the computer analogy to make some sense of what the brain does. Like a computer it carries out whatever it is programmed to do. If you type a document using a word processing program and make an error in the content, it still gets printed unless you change what you typed. The software program doesn't evaluate your text or content. It publishes it exactly as you instruct it to. It saves it in whatever form you save it.

The hardware of your computer uses software programs to execute tasks. These do whatever they are designed to do. If it is working you don't type the word 'rabbit' and get 'planet mars' you get the word 'rabbit'. It works this way without fail. It is reliable. It is consistent. You don't even have to think about it.

The brain learns from exposure and experience through repetition. Anything you repeat long enough, becomes a habit. It doesn't matter if it is good or bad or right or wrong. That is why you may have a supportive habit such as brushing your teeth daily or making your bed, or you may have destructive habits such as smoking or biting your nails.

You brain doesn't evaluate whether these are good or bad, or right or wrong. It just continues to do what it has learned to do.

Once it learns what to do, it attempts to continue to make it happen. This is homeostasis. An example of homeostasis is how your thermostat works in your home. If you set it to 70 degrees and it gets warmer than 70 it stops putting out heat. If the temperature falls below 70 degrees the heat kicks on. It does this to maintain the setting. Homeostasis means to keep things the same.

Your brain works similarly to maintain the settings it has acquired or learned. Brains are learning machines. Whenever you learn something you actually grow and lay down neural pathways and networks in the brain. You inner 'servo-mechanism' works day and night to keep you the same. It keeps you consistent. That is what habits do. You don't have to think about them, you just do them.

The brain uses these pathways and networks repeatedly unless another pathway redirects it. Brains learn by generalization. Once you learn how to open a door, or sit on a chair your brain generalizes that learning to all other recognizable doors and chairs. You do not have to relearn how to do these behaviors once you have already learned them.

The brain streamlines. Here is an example. You live in your house or apartment. You learned how to get to and from there. You know the address and all the routes. Then you move to a new place. You leave work or school for the new place. Instead of going there, you find yourself at the old home. That is your brain carrying out what it learned to do.

You go to your previous home because that is what you were conditioned to do. You may do this a number of times until the brain learns the new route to the new address. It never forgets the old but it eventually replaces it.

Because you never forget, is why you can get back on and ride a bicycle, no matter how long it has been since you rode one. Your brain has stored the information and pathways for how to ride it. You may need a little re-acquaintance time but you will be able to ride it again. This is true about many things we have learned to do.

While growing up you were exposed to numerous behaviors, beliefs, concepts, thoughts and emotions from your family, peers and friends, educators, others, the media and entertainment. You were repeatedly exposed to these beliefs, which got wired in as neural pathways or habitual thought, feeling and behavioral habits or patterns.

Some of the beliefs or concepts you learned were, whether or not the world is a friendly or hostile place, or both; you learned whether money is good and easy to come by, or whether it is evil and hard to make and hold on to. You learned whether you are deserving, smart, lovable, and talented, or not so much. You learned to respect yourself and others, or any number of variations.

These things you learned and these thought habits, constitute your beliefs. While learning beliefs you learned values, too. Values are those concepts and principles that are important to you, like freedom, money, fun, power, love, family, honesty, loyalty, integrity and more. You spend you energy, time and money trying to attain and maintain values because you BELIEVE these are important to you. Get it? Your personality, many of your values, and the bulk of your beliefs, habits and feeling habits were laid down by the time you were about seven.

From that point on most of what we do, researchers claim, is between 95 and 99% habitual, automatic programmed thinking, feeling and behaving. We get upset the same way about different things. We fall in love the same way with different people or things. We have the same problems over and over. We date or marry the same type of person. We have similar money issues all our lives unless we change it. Unfortunately, many people never do.

The good news is we can change it. We can reprogram our brains but we have to reprogram them the same way they were originally programmed by consistent repetition over a period of time. Only, today, we now choose to do it consciously. This is an important point to understand!

Now, let's return to survival. Your brain, your Reticular Activating System (RAS), is the brain's center for attention. It is the place your inner thoughts and feelings converge with outside influences. It has two primary functions.

One: It is designed to look for what is wrong in your environment in order to help you survive. It evolved to help you avoid being eaten. It notices what is wrong or different around you so you can escape or fight or freeze, if necessary.

The RAS resides at the base of the skull. It works in tandem with the amygdala, which is the part of your limbic system within the brain that is responsible for emotions, survival and memories.

It is designed to keep you the same. To keep you surviving as you are. Whenever a change occurs the RAS can feel threatened. It works to maintain your thermostat setting, otherwise known as homeostasis. It tries to keep you as you are instead of as you may want to be. Change is perceived as a threat. That is the reason you may feel uncomfortable with some changes you want to make.

You may try to lose weight but eventually give up. You want to wake up early but you keep sleeping in. You promise you won't yell at the kids but you keep doing it. Your brain, your subconscious keeps reverting back to the old, to keep you as you are. Get it? It only knows what it knows to do. It doesn't judge, so it does it reliably and automatically.

It keeps us the same through discomfort. You don't feel like it BUT actually it is your friend! It is attempting to keep you consistent and alive. It doesn't realize you may want other things from what you previously learned. Understand this! In order to change your programming, you need to update it.

Two: The RAS looks for matches. It looks for what is the same. It searches for and finds memories, associations and experiences inside of you and events and circumstances in the outer world that are important to you. Since it looks for matches in the environment and within your memories or experiences, or mental associations, what-ever you focus on you will get more of.

If something isn't important to you it is unlikely you will notice it. It doesn't have a high enough signal value for your attention. Once it becomes important to you, you notice it more often.

For example you buy a brand new car. Prior to purchasing it you did not notice that type of car on the roadway much. NOW that it is yours and important to you, you see the same make and model everywhere. Your brain is finding them for you. They were always there. You just hadn't noticed.

This is why, what you focus on is what you get. If you ask yourself why you are such an idiot you brain will find all the examples it can in response. It will find matches of when and where you behaved as such. If you say, 'how come I am so brilliant', you brain will find those matches, too. Whichever you ask more of, more often, your brain is more used to going and finding those matches immediately.

It travels those familiar neural pathways. If you have more difficulty thinking positively than negatively, it is only because you have traveled the negative pathways more frequently. Your RAS has found those matches more regularly. This is why you are reading this book to learn to master your thought habits!

To make a change you need to reroute. You need to re-think. You need to choose what you want your brain to do for you. You need to stop traveling to the old (like the old address) and start traveling to the new. If you criticize yourself a lot, you need to stop it. You need to begin praising yourself.

That will seem tough, uncomfortable and you may not want to do it. That is your brain attempting to keep you the same. In order to get used to the new thoughts, feelings and behaviors you have to repeat the new thought, feeling and behavior, again and again, until it becomes a new replacement habit.

Get it? It is a conditioning process. A re-conditioning process you consciously decide to do. Once you begin replacing the old habits with new habits you evolve into the person you want to be. You begin to break free of the old conditioning you learned as a child.

You can change your thoughts and feelings about yourself. You can overcome bad habits. You can learn to make more money, fall in love, enjoy healthy relationships, lose weight, get fit and live life according to your terms.

Once you reprogram your brain for new positive thoughts and behaviors you brain automatically scans for those. You begin to become aware of opportunities you never previously noticed, just like that car you bought. Your RAS works to help you succeed because you program your servo-mechanism to help you succeed.

Frankly, your brain doesn't care what you program, or whether it is negative or positive, but, you do, you consciously care. It doesn't, subconsciously. It will continue to smoke because that is what it learned to do. YOU want to quit. You need to LEARN that you are directing an incredibly powerful servant that can only say yes. The power of 95-99% subconscious, automated, habitual, reliable programming is at your disposal.

Once you get it on your side (and it doesn't choose or care) it is yours forever. If you hadn't decided to quit smoking, or make a positive change, it would continue on, with the same old habits, forever. It doesn't care! You will always be as you were, unless you change it.

Do you get this? It is important to understand. When you begin the process of deliberately taking control of your own mind you will wage a battle with inertia. You will need to overcome subconscious habits you may have had for many years. Recall what I wrote about discomfort. You will face this, too. Get over it!

The great news is YOU ABSOLUTELY CAN!!! Bit by bit. Inch by inch you can make tremendous headway and succeed in ways you could never, ever begin to imagine. Some things take longer than others. Some things happen instantly.

Originally, your subconscious mind was programmed without your conscious approval. Now, in order to change, you need to consciously decide to reprogram your subconscious mind to work for you in the ways you want it to. That's what the principles and practices I share with you will help you to do.

You can evolve and transform yourself in positive and powerful ways. You can change limiting beliefs into powerful beliefs that support you in being, doing and having what you want. You can get rid of blockages and bothersome feelings. You can eliminate negativity and become a powerhouse of positivity with the ability to move forward. You will begin to think, 'I CAN DO THIS' instead of, 'I can't.'

When you apply the principles and practices I share with you, and make them habits, you will learn you can overcome most any challenge and find ways to make your dreams come true. Countless others have in my workshops and from my writing. You can too!

You will stop whining and start winning! You will stop living as a victim and start living as a victor. You'll become a champion and design the life of your dreams. You will start living on your terms.

NOTE: PLEASE READ

This book utilizes whole-brain and accelerated learning concepts. It may not read like a book you're used to. I've used certain conventions to encourage you to go back and re-read sentences and paragraphs over again to increase your understanding. There's lots of repetition! Lots of repetition to expose your mind to important concepts. Some punctuation and lack of it, underlining, bold words and CAPS may seem odd. That's okay. The bold headlines may or may not seem to support the chapter material. It's all intentional. Think, re-read, review and reflect on what you read. Consider this a workbook for making yourself and your life wonderful and not a typical book or novel you read. Think of it as listening to me, a caring friend, whispering in your ear. I am speaking to both your conscious and non-conscious. Release concern about how a book should read. Let go, listen, learn and enjoy this process.

"Self-pity is the worst possible emotion anyone can have. It's the most destructive. It destroys everything around it, except itself!" — Stephen Fry

"You are essentially who you create yourself to be and all that occurs in your life is the result of your own making." — Stephen Richards

"What would you do if you weren't afraid?" — Sheryl Sandberg

IMPORTANT NOTE

In 2007 neuroscientist, Norman Doidge, shared an important finding with the world in his book, *The Brain That Changes Itself*. He and other researchers since have determined that "the brain can change its own structure and function through thought and activity."

This is incredible news because science confirmed what the ancient wise ones already seemed to know and suggest. Doidge heralded this discovery as "the most important alteration in our view of the brain since we first sketched out its basic anatomy and the workings of its basic component, the neuron."

In workshops, I conducted alone and together with other co-trainers in the early 80's, I suggested that anyone could grow new neural pathways and evolve their brain. At times we were ridiculed as charlatans. Mystics of course, have known this for eons.

Today, it is called "neuroplasticity" and it means the brain can adapt and evolve depending on how we use it. We can make it better or worse. It can be enhanced through positive thinking and feeling. Stress and less than glorious emotions and experiences, can hamper it.

The great news is, though, hampered, at any time, the adaptability of the brain means we can overcome all sorts of, previously thought, obstacles and limitations. We are not stuck with the intelligence and tendencies we developed as children. We are not victims of habit, or of a neurology that can't change. We can change! We can absolutely change it!

This is fantastic news for you and me. Positive thinking and positive practices have positive impact and they work. Positive mental and physical conditioning makes a difference. Meditation and positive reflection heals the brain. You can overcome stress and debilitating sadness, anger, fear or worry by learning to condition your brain for positive, healthy thoughts and feelings. Ask any of my students.

Not only can you absolutely train your brain, you can change your brain! You can make it work for you and support you. You can make an unhealthy brain, healthier again.

This is potentially, great news for those who have suffered other forms of trauma, abuse and brain damage. As, it relates to you and me, we can change and evolve ourselves, physically and mentally, to become the people we want to be. It isn't magic. It is brain science.

"Once you start laughing, you start healing." — *Sherry Argov*

CHAPTER ONE

You Can Do Anything

In your hands or on your device you hold a most important document. The life-changing methods I share come from my online programs and workshops. This book was written using the best principles and practices I've shared for 40 years to help you MAKE PERMANENT the POSITIVE CHANGES you want to make in your life. My goal is to help you to achieve your goals, live your passion and make your dreams come true as I have for countless others. As they have YOU can too! You can get great results!

My work, this book, will challenge you. This book will change you. I will provoke you to go beyond what you already know. To gain the most benefit from this book I encourage you to stay open-minded. In fact, I insist on it. Still, that will be completely up to you. Too many of us think we are open-minded. Sadly, we are not.

Three of the most dangerous words humans can think or say are, "I know that". The moment those words are thought, the brain shuts down. It retreats into what was and is not available instead of into what is or what can be. Thinking, "I know that" reduces everything to "I've been there and done that. There is nothing new for me here". The truth is just the opposite! There is so much here. I want you to get it!

You Can Do Most Anything When You Believe You Can

Nuance makes an incredible difference. Amazingly talented artists are able to make use of color, light and shadow, texture, hue and saturation in ways most of us never consider. Whether we appreciate the final work or not the hours that go into making that artwork can be numerous. The artist works with numerous distinctions the rest of us may miss.

We look at the finished work and think, "Wow, cool." We don't notice all there is in it. We don't know all of the work that went into it. Most of us travel the world with blinders on. We do. All of us! We don't notice what we don't notice. We think we are aware of most of it, but we aren't. Yet, we still think we're open.

Our brains can only consciously process a limited amount of information. We become aware only of a teeny, tiny, itsy-bitsy, sliver or fragment of information while sifting through trillions of bits of data at the subconscious level outside of our awareness. We don't notice much!

Realize It Is All In Your Mind

Most of what we see, hear and think is determined by habit. We were conditioned to notice what we noticed and miss what we missed while we were growing up. So when you think, "I know that" realize you will miss a great deal that is there. A great deal you never normally consider.

The second you say it you slam the door shut. I urge you, keep the door open. Work at it. You will have to. To become aware you must become aware that you weren't and aren't aware. You first need to realize when you are preoccupied and missing something. Then, work to change it. STAY OPEN! OPEN UP!

You need to BECOME AWARE of when you close your mind to new ideas or ones different than what you are used to. Awareness is the first practice you must adopt in order to change. Without it you won't get very far. You'll keep missing out on everything you already have been missing.

Spend Time Uplifting Others

My motto is "exploration is the doorway to adventure and curiosity the key". When you are curious you are seeking. You are willing to be OPEN AND AVAILABLE. A child can watch a butterfly with rapt attention and fascination for an endless amount of time. Be as a little child. Be open. Be playful. Explore.

Adventure! I challenge you to remain open to learn new things and about things you think you already know. I'll invite you to try on new thoughts, ideas, feelings and behaviors. I mean really try them on as you would try on new clothing or shoes. Test them out. Wear them a while. Get comfortable with them.

I invite you to implement what you learn mentally. Put it into action. Bring it to life. Unless you play the game you will never really know the game. Yes, you can watch it and learn the rules but if you don't play the game, you won't truly know it. I invite you to play. Play full-on 100%.

You Can Direct Your Mind And Your Heart

Try on the new clothes; decide if they fit and if you like them. How do you look in them? Realize, when you first try something on you never had before, your immediate tendency may be, to exclaim "Nah, this isn't me". Then remove them. It might be, it could be you. You just aren't used to it, yet.

Why not? You already have your style. You have what you are used to. You have what you are comfortable with. You have your set image and style locked in already. If I dressed you in a white Elvis Presley sequin jumpsuit you might argue that just isn't you. Yet, he made it work.

You could too but only if you ALLOW YOURSELF to feel completely at home in it. That means putting it on and wearing it until you are comfortable with it. Wear it until it is you. If he could, then you can. The question is; will you give it a try? If you won't, then you will never know. That is being closed, not open.

Like Attracts Like

You have to be willing to leave your comfort zone and go beyond what you already know and feel is right. It is that simple. It is that necessary. It is that important! I'll never ask you to sacrifice your integrity but I will ask you to explore new, novel ideas and practices. Some of which, you may already be familiar with. Re-visit these again and do it with A NEW MINDSET and outlook.

To really excel, all of us need to stay open and have a great attitude toward learning new things.

Your attitude toward learning is the most important predictor for a successful learning outcome. If you consider learning and applying this material fun and exciting, your outcome will be positive. One of the many research studies that concluded this was a cancer study.

Travis Air Force Base studied 152 cancer patients and their treatments. The results demonstrated that the "attitude toward treatment was a better predictor of response to treatment than was the severity of the disease." That means the outcome was determined by the patient's attitude to the treatment and not how bad the illness was. That is pretty impressive, don't you think? Attitude makes a big, big difference!

If learning or staying open for you has been difficult in the past, change it now. This is your opportunity.

A Mind Stretched Can Never Go Back To Its Original Dimension

Get it? If you always do what you have always done you will continue to get what you always got. You won't get new things. To be new, you need to DO NEW THINGS!

If you always plant beans you won't one day get corn. You will continue to get the beans you plant. In order to change your life you must change what you are doing. Some people continue to do the same things, thinking they will get different results and that is just plain crazy.

"Insane" they call it. Still, many people don't realize that in order to do something new, you actually have to DO SOMETHING NEW. So stay open. Be willing to be uncomfortable. Remain open. Dive in. Analyze later. Analyze after the fact. Stop analyzing before you do it. It doesn't help. Do it first!

Realize It Is All In Your Mind

You can't know something before you know it. Many people are afraid to dive in. They fear going for it. Once they dive in they think, "That wasn't so bad. That was FUN. Let's do it again." At worst they go, "Wow I will never do that again," but at least they did.

From experience they make a decision. They did it! Fear prevents most people from trying new things. They are afraid they will fail. Perhaps, they are afraid they will succeed. They are afraid they won't like it or perhaps that they will. The reasons may be countless. Analyzing without experiencing won't teach you.

The result is the same. Whatever stops you; does so, until it doesn't any longer. Once stopped, you aren't going anywhere until you get into motion. Fear is the equivalent of being stopped, all wheels spinning but not making contact with the road. Lot's of busy-ness but no progress.

Whom Do You Spend Most Time With

People waste time being afraid. Courage isn't the absence of fear. Courage is doing it even while afraid. Some people are afraid to speak in front of groups. Some people speak in front of groups even though it scares them. They simply manage their fears and DO IT anyway.

Few of us ever get eaten by lions, tigers or bears. Yet, we think that is what happens. I mean really. If we stand in front of others and talk what is the absolute worst that could happen? Someone thinks you are an idiot? No one likes it, or you? Some strangers don't care for you. Really, what is the very worst thing?

We don't face survival fears as our ancestors did. We face imaginary fears mostly. We live in artificially lit boxes and drive in protective boxes to and from one fairly cushy box place to another. We are not out hunting, foraging for food, nor braving the elements and wild animals. We think and act as if we were.

Which Are You – Builder OR Destroyer

We aren't! At the worst we may feel stupid, embarrassed, and not liked. At worst we take an emotional hit. While this may not be desirable it isn't the worst that could happen. Do you UNDER-STAND THIS? You know this right? There are worse things. Fear, over-analysis and worry are only bad habits!

Most people make the fear of trying new things unrealistic. That's because they have done the same thing over and over for so long it is habit. Because it is habit it seems hard to get over. They continue with it in spite of not wanting to and not liking it. Most people don't know how to change.

Not only do they not know how, but also they are afraid to try. It isn't that difficult or scary. They just think it is. It is a limitation all in the mind. They think it is hard, so it is. They think it is scary, so it is.

I am not going to spend much, if any time, going over how we got "stuck" or "broken" in the first place. Suffice to say we were born, and we grew up. Along the way we were exposed to thoughts and experiences that formed the basis for our beliefs and values, our talents and our limitations. We learn habits of thought, feeling and behavior that serve and support us or hold us back and make us feel bad.

This book is about how you can change all that. Changing and transforming yourself is the focus, not the conditions or initial causes. Get it? We move forward. You become free of the old and move into the new.

Be A Beacon And You Will Attract The Best

You can change anything and overcome anything given two things.

1. Make it manageable. Break it into tiny, doable pieces.

2. Give yourself enough time. Step by step, in time, you will get there.

Stop saying "no." Stop saying "I know that." STAY OPEN! Say "yes." Say, "I will try it on! I will practice it. I will do it until I discover the difference that makes a difference." Be willing to try. Attempt it, for goodness sake! Be willing to go for it. Relax about it and get excited!

Thoughts Become Things

Your first exercise is coming up. Are you willing to PLAY and LEARN? If so, here it is, but first, a story.

Are you familiar with the story of the Zen disciple and the teacup? The young disciple asks the Master to share his knowledge with him. The Master gives him a teacup and asks if he would like to join the Master for some tea. Of course he would.

The Master pours. The cup fills. The tea overflows the cup onto the floor. The Master continues to pour and pour. "STOP!" Exclaims the disciple. "The cup is full." The Master states, "Your cup is full. In order to learn you must first empty your cup. Go away. When you are empty, you may return."

Energy Flows Where Your Attention Goes

Exercise: Part 1. Go back and reread everything you read so far with a new awareness and openness. Think how it can be possible to change and be a new person. Get curious. Become fascinated. Enjoy. For anything, you said, "I know that, already" empty your cup, your mind, and say, "Wow, interesting, I did not know this". Empty your cup. Stay open!

Part 2. Stay as open as you can as you continue to read through this book. With each and every concept you think you already know, say, "Wow, interesting, I didn't know that." Get curious. BECOME FASCINATED. See if you can go beyond what you already know. Enjoy this process. Use it to go beyond and into new areas of discovery that can be rich for you, beyond belief. And now…

"An open mind leaves a chance for someone to drop a worthwhile thought in it."
— *Mark Twain*

"It is only when the correct practice is followed for a long time, without interruptions and with a quality of positive attitude and eagerness, that it can succeed."
— *Patanjali*

"Be thankful for what you have and you'll wind up having more. If you concentrate on what you don't have you will never have enough."
— *Oprah Winfrey*

"The positive thinker sees the invisible, feels the intangible, and achieves the impossible."
— *Anonymous*

CHAPTER TWO

The Misconception About Motivation

GET EAGER FOR CHANGE. Change can be scary but it can also be massive fun and inspiring. It can be motivating. It can be thrilling! Many people wait until they feel motivated to do something. That rarely works. They use negative pressure in order to get going. Deadlines help do that.

They use the stick approach. If it gets bad enough they will move. You might dally around the forest never feeling like you have to leave. If a bear chased you, I bet you'd get moving! You'd be motivated to go! Some people only move when it gets really bad. You hear it all the time, "No pain, No gain". It is a belief. Part of a limiting mindset that infers you don't change unless it hurts. That is bull!

Many people use pain to motivate themselves. They wait until the last minute and then stress about it. Have you ever done this? If you want to continue doing that to yourself that is your choice. I say, STOP IT! There is another way. Motivation, true motivation, actually comes from doing.

Direct Your Thoughts And Feelings

When you do things, when you TAKE ACTION, you actually begin to get more motivated to continue to do them. Don't miss out on an important point here. Motivation doesn't come from waiting. It isn't fun when it is painful. There is another way. Act first and motivation follows!

You have been putting the cart before the horse if you are like most people. You have been waiting until you feel like it. That isn't how it works. You do it first and the motivated feeling will follow. Champion athletes often don't feel like training day to day but they DO IT anyway.

They know if they do it now there is the potential reward later. They know if they don't act now that reward is unlikely to ever be theirs. They train now, when they don't feel like they want to. They do it anyway. Once at the gym or outside training they feel much more like continuing. It works! This IS the way it works. You need to understand this. Motivation arrives after you act. It doesn't come before action.

Choose Positive OR Negative

Muhammad Ali, one of the world's champion boxers, stated "I hated every minute of training, but I said, 'Don't quit. Suffer now and live the rest of your life as a champion.'" He trained, though he didn't feel like it because the end result was worth it. His "why are you doing this" was a big enough desire. Get it? He had POWER-FUL, big enough, reasons to do it. You can bet he felt glad he completed each day of training when the session was over.

It works this way. DOING the task PRODUCES the MOTIVA-TION to keep on going. Action produces the feeling. Nowhere is it written, that in order to do things you must first feel like it. That is crappy thinking. Do it! The results will follow. Do it! You will reap the reward. Do it! Do it! Do it!

The other way to get yourself motivated is to consider your "big reasons" for doing it, just as Muhammad Ali did. If the reward is great then it is worth making it happen now. Find big enough, important reasons that provide you the motivation, the impetus to take the actions you need to.

Yet, many people are like the frog in the pot of water. It's a sad, but true, fact. This is an example.

Do not do this! It is cruel. A frog placed in a pot with water will remain in the pot while the temperature is increased. It will remain there not realizing what is happening until it is too late.

It adjusts its body temperature with the changing water temperature. Throw a frog into a boiling pot and it would scramble to get out! Again, this is a sad, but true illustration. Many people are the same way. They don't notice, nor do anything, until it is already too late. Once it gets really bad, they might act. Then, they mostly whine and complain.

They make excuses for themselves. They blame the world, outer circumstances and others for their troubles. Stop! Take responsibility for yourself! TAKE RESPONSIBILITY for changing your life and your future. Initiate the changes by remaining open and doing new things.

Take Responsibility

KEEP PRACTICING them until you make new habits. Your new habits will REPLACE THE OLD. It will take some time, so hang in there. Step by step you will get there. It won't take too long but it will require some time and you must stick with it. If you quit or dabble, don't expect much.

Do you know most people don't read self-help books past the first chapter? Don't let that be you. Be different. Be one of the far fewer numbers of people who go for their dreams and keep going and doing until they accomplish them. You can MAKE YOUR DREAMS COME TRUE. It starts within you. It begins with your thoughts and leads to your actions.

You can be an absolutely brand new you if you do the exercises in this book. This material can revolutionize your life. If you don't put it to use, if you don't immediately ACT on this information, it will remain information.

What You Resist Persists

You will have been exposed to some life-changing ideas and practices, that could change your life, but they will just remain great ideas. Act on them. I repeat, act on them! Implement them and you will transform! Practice! Act quickly. Act within 48 hours of being exposed to this material.

COMMIT to doing it right away. Train your brain that you keep your word. If you put it off, and someday get around to it, you train your brain to do nothing but wait. Don't you think you have waited long enough? DO IT NOW. When you act right away, you tell your brain this is important and so am I!

Make new supportive habits and you will revolutionize your life. YOU WILL CHANGE because YOU are doing them. Change won't happen to you.

Change will happen because of you. HAVE FUN. Be excited. Take it lightly and take it seriously, but not too seriously .

Stay open and delighted. Live, love, laugh and learn today!"

Turn Resistance Into Assistance

Take it seriously enough to keep doing it and light enough to enjoy it. It can be uncomfortable facing and changing old thoughts feelings and behavioral habits. It can also be wildly freeing and awe-inspiring! You can FEEL FREE AND CONFIDENT. You can fall in love with life.

You will be able to ELIMINATE UNWANTED HABITS and SOLVE PROBLEMS. You will learn you can create, design and live the life you always have wanted to. It is completely up to you. YOU will be making it happen. I will be your guide but you must take the journey with me.

I'll point out the sights and pathways but you have to see them and take them. I can't do it for you. If you will do it, the future is yours. DECIDE NOW, THIS IS RIGHT FOR YOU. Then claim it. Make your tomorrows your todays. Begin to live that successful future you, right now. Don't wait. ENGAGE.

The Question Is More Important Than An Answer

Put all four wheels on the ground and BEGIN MOVING. Yes, today can be the first day of the rest of your new, exciting, adventurous, happy and prosperous life. Make it so! Stay open and delighted.

"We are so accustomed to the comforts of "I cannot", "I do not want to" and "it is too difficult" that we forget to realize when we stop doing things for ourselves and expect others to dance around us, we are not achieving greatness. We have made ourselves weak."
— *Pandora Poikilos*

"The prison of the past is one you must escape in order to pivot. Our job now is to find out where your attachments to the past lie."
— *Adam Markel*

"The moment you change your perceptions is the moment you rewrite your body chemistry."
— *Bruce Lipton*

"I am happy and I think being happy really keeps you looking young."
— *Olivia Newton John*

CHAPTER THREE

There's No Such Thing As 'Self-Sabotage'

In my programs people first are surprised to learn this. Then they embrace it. You can too. When people attempt to make a career or personal change, but aren't successful, they sometimes believe, somehow, they sabotaged it. You want to lose weight but you ate that donut, right? Can we ever stop screwing it up? It seems as if something is working against your best intentions. Is it self-sabotage? Why on Earth does this happen?

Do you know why you are you told it is important to THINK POSITIVE? The reason you think positive is to keep your mind occupied with positive thoughts. That is why people AFFIRM, watch their self-talk and change it to the positive when they notice it is less than glorious; to fill their minds with good things; to exclude the negative and what they don't want. It's important to keep your mind filled right!

That is why they chant affirmations and mantras, read inspiring books, put posters and mottos up around their environment, listen to positive and motivational audios, hang with other positive people and attend live events. DO THESE THINGS so that most of your waking hours are spent thinking and feeling good. If you don't do these, change and begin now. Keep yourself oriented to the positive and what you can do!

Your Subconscious Programming Daily Checklist:

1. Chant affirmations and mantras enthusiastically

2. Read positive, inspiring and motivational books

3. Put posters and mottos up around your environment

4. Listen to positive, inspiring and motivational audios

5. Hang out with other positive people

6. Attend live events, classes, seminars and training

Your Thoughts Determine Your Outcomes

Keep your mind positively occupied most of the time because when you do you FEEL BETTER. Then the preponderance of your day is spent less negative, more positive and more OPTIMISTIC. You complain and gripe less and look on the bright side more. Instead of problems, issues, gossip and negative distractions, you look at solutions and what is possible. Your FOCUS is on what works. As you do this, you REPROGRAM your subconscious mind.

Your subconscious relies on the signals, or messages you send it. It pays attention to the highest emotional signal value and what you concentrate on most of the time. What you focus on expands. What you think about and FEEL strongly about, you bring about. Your subconscious responds to how you feel!

Your subconscious mind is your servo-mechanism. That means friend. It is your friend, your reliable supportive ally. It says, "YES" to anything you say, whether positive or negative. It agrees with your thoughts and inner statements no matter what they are. It looks for a match in the outer world of results for what you already BELIEVE. It keeps you the same. It keeps you consistent. It is loyal to who you are.

Your subconscious mind streamlines things for you so you don't have to relearn everything. It is your best friend. This is good news, especially if you weren't told this before! Yet, sadly, most people get it wrong. They claim your subconscious is against you; that it harbors beliefs and paradigms that make it difficult for you to change. That is just plain wrong. It is incorrect. It is untrue!

Your subconscious is a learning machine! Everything you know how to THINK and do, it learned for you. Everything you do, POSITIVE or negative, good or bad, it learned to do and to keep doing it. It will keep doing it unless you change it. It is a reliable and faithful servant. These 'so-called experts' tell you it is sabotaging you. It isn't! It is serving you!

It is supporting you with what it learned to do. IF you want your subconscious to do something different for you, you have to tell it what you want. You need to train it to DO THE NEW THINGS, the same way it learned to do the many old things, it already does.

What You Hold In Your Mind You Can Hold In Your Hand

How did it learn what it learned? It learned through repetition and emotion. That's how! Do, repeat, do and repeat. It learned from repeated exposure and experience. Repetition builds habits.

The issue for most people is that they let their brains run on without ever taking charge of it. They are not in control. They are passengers and their brain is doing the driving. They are in the backseat of a car and go wherever the driver takes them. They aren't driving the vehicle. They are being transported.

Your brain transports you and drives you unless, and until, you ASSUME CONTROL. It does this because it is your friend. It does what it learned to do reliably so the trip is comfortable and familiar.

It doesn't want to rock your world or scare you. It serves you as it best knows how. It keeps everything the same for you. Consistent! It takes care of you! It wants you to remain the same. No matter what.

You Are Where Your Thoughts Take You

Since most people have been told change is hard, they assume that is the truth. Our inner expectations determine what we tend to find in the outer world. Our brain seeks a match for what we already accept as true. So if we assume change is difficult, that is what we will find. In reality, it isn't always easy, but it isn't hard. Any person can LEARN TO CHANGE!

Your brain learns easily and readily. It learned all kinds of wonderful and useful things. It learned all sorts of useless and less than glorious things. To TRANSFORM YOURSELF you want to remove or replace the less than glorious, useless programming, with more positive, productive, useful, glorious programming. You simply, switch one for the other.

Many people learned to focus on problems, limitations and issues. They focus on debt, poor health, trouble and calamity, instead of what they want. That is what they learned to do. The reason they never get out of debt or their health never improves is that they continue doing the same things in the same way, habitually. They don't change anything!

They want to be different but they keep doing what they have already done and then hope it will be better. Unfortunately, that does not work. Then they blame themselves, others, god, the world, circumstances and the environment. They only need to MAKE A FEW SIMPLE CHANGES. If they did, everything could begin to change!

A few simple changes and they could be well on their way to an incredible new life. Sadly, most stop there. They say they tried and it didn't work. They quit. Throw in the towel. Do you know when most people actually quit? Before they ever try anything. They think it will be too hard and they talk themselves out of it. It is true. They quit early. We learned all these things, good and bad growing up.

Skill Comes From Doing

Have you ever done that? I sure have, in the past. Why do we do that? We quit before we try or we try and quit quickly. Our culture tells us to. We have popular phrases. "Three strikes and you're out." "If at first you don't succeed, try, try again." Then what? Then quit! We have been conditioned to try a few times and give up. Argh! Abandon the pursuit.

The reality is you must keep going until you break through. Consider this amazing fact. People have tunneled out of prison using only a spoon. Can you IMAGINE THAT? Certainly, if they gave up after weeks or even months they'd never have gotten out. You have to keep going until you break free. If you really want it! You must commit and persist to making the changes you want, if you want to make them.

A few simple changes are all it takes to begin to RECONDITION YOUR SUBCONSCIOUS to do what you want it to do. If your lover constantly did something that annoyed you, or hurt you, wouldn't you attempt to explain to them there was a better way they could treat you? You have to TELL YOUR SUBCONSCIOUS there is a new way you prefer. It loves to learn! You have to communicate with it.

Ask Yourself Questions

You have to communicate with it the way it understands. Give it the new task of learning to BE MORE POSITIVE. Tell it you want to be a new, positive, productive, incredible you! Educate it. It knows how to learn. You don't have to teach it that. It uses repetition and emotion to learn new skills. You need to provide what it should learn. You need to tell it, you are a positive person!

"I want to be happy." "I want to be financially free." There are ways to instruct your brain so you get what you want. Right now, people are instructing their brains to give them more of what they precisely don't want. They THINK about, fret over, worry and concentrate on exactly what they want to avoid or exclude. This only gets them more of the very same things they do not want and wish to eliminate.

They negatively focus. The only message the brain gets over and over again, is what they are focused on. "I don't want to be poor." "I have lots of bills." "I am in so much debt." "My back hurts." "The tumor has grown." "I am so unhappy." "I am worried." "I am stupid." "I am worthless." "I can't do things right." "I could never learn that." "Some people are lucky but not me." "Why do bad things always happen?"

If You Think You Can Or You Think You Can't You Are Right

All of those statements create negative images in one's mind, not only negative images but also really negative, crummy feelings. The thoughts and pictures and feelings are negative and unwanted. Your subconscious doesn't make the distinction between POSITIVE or negative and good or bad. It only gets what you send it with highest signal value. In each sentence notice what the main word is that stands out. The words most readily noticed are: poor, bills, debt, back or hurts, tumor, unhappy, worried, stupid, and so on. What do these words make you picture or feel? That is what you are telling your brain you want! Yuk!

Celebrate Learn From And Let Go Of The Past

The main word and the feeling that comes from it, is what occupies the mind. If you took all of the other words away, you are left with a less than glorious concept, or picture in your mind and negative or bad feelings. Here are some of the words: debt, bills, poor, tumor, and unhappy. Those are the message!

Whatever you FOCUS on expands. Worse yet, people think these same thoughts over and over. Imagine, how you might feel if this is the way you think most of the time. This is self-fulfilling prophecy! Get it?

It is a negative loop. The subconscious repeats things reliably from habit. That is what it does! You get more of the same crappy thoughts, feelings and results in your life. You don't want that to continue, do you?

Good Questions Produce Good Results

If there are times in your life that have sucked in the past; if you have lived less than glorious days; if some of the life you have lived you didn't consciously want, then you <u>already</u> have proof that your mind brings about those things you concentrate on. If you have struggled to get out of debt only to keep incurring more, you have the proof. What more evidence do you want that you are a creator?

You get whatever you focus on. GOOD or bad, positive or negative, you are creating it subconsciously. The 'so-called experts' call it sabotage. It is just your subconscious taking instructions from your thoughts and feelings. It is just your friend doing what it thinks you want and carrying out what it has learned to do. It is serving you the way it learned while you were too little to care or do it for yourself. It did it.

It does it to serve you. <u>You</u> have already proved it to yourself when you got the results you didn't want, and you keep getting those same results over and over again. You have conditioned yourself for those.

Whatever you focus on with emotion is the message. What you THINK AND FEEL over and over again, most of the time, <u>is</u> what you send your subconscious. It is what you AFFIRM, assert and declare and FEEL that makes the most impact. People feel bad about debt, bills, tumors and unhappiness. Get it?

The Past Brought You To Now

You don't want the negative stuff but your unconscious mind thinks you do because you keep focusing on it and <u>feeling</u> it. That is the message it gets. You keep sending a shabby message to it.

Through constant repetition of thoughts and <u>feelings</u> you tell your subconscious mind what is important and what it should pay attention to. What happens if large portions of your day are spent thinking or worrying about bills and scarcity while other portions of your day are spent in mindless distractions and negative Internet news items? What is the bulk of your thinking throughout the day? Hmmmmm?

What is the predominant message your subconscious gets? The message it gets is, "More bills, more bills, more bills, things suck, more bills, more bills, more bills. Scarcity. I feel crappy." Get it? Do you understand? You think crappy and feel crappy all day long. Your subconscious gets the message!

If You Really Want Something You Will Find A Way

Over and over during the day 'bills' is what you fretted over. You were preoccupied and anxious about them. You were concerned. You felt crummy. Your subconscious goes, "Okay I get what you deem is important. I'll take care of you. Here have some more!" The other times during your day were 'whatever moments', daily distractions and traffic woes, meaningless meanderings, etc. These don't count!

Your subconscious looks to create or find a match for what is MOST IMPORTANT to you. It is trying to help. It really IS trying to help! It is! It thinks you want to focus on bills because that IS what you focused on mostly. That is what you are emotional about. That is where you spend most of your time. You feel it!

It is not your subconscious' fault you sent it crappy, unwanted instructions. Then you blame it for sabotaging you. Shame! It carries out your orders precisely. It gives you more of what you focused on the most. That's how IT works! That IS all it knows. It is simply saying 'YES' to you! You sent the message!

Drop By Drop The Tub Fills

If you didn't mean to send that message, and even though you didn't know any better, it is giving you exactly what it <u>thinks</u> you want. Only, <u>you</u> consciously, don't want it. Do you get this, yet?

49

If you blame your subconscious for sabotaging you, when it is really only trying to do your bidding, it is like slapping yourself in the face. It is not much different than rebuking a child for doing exactly what you told the child to do. When you blame and criticize yourself this way you get worse results not better.

When you harbor the belief that you are capable of sabotaging yourself, you are, in essence saying, that part of you is trying to harm all of you. You'll foul up future attempts, to get what you want, because you don't even TRUST, like or RESPECT YOUR-SELF. You are at odds with you. Stop this. End that now.

We Always Have Been Creating Only Now We Direct The Process

Instead you need to LOVE YOURSELF. Accept yourself. Allow yourself to be who you are with all of the imperfections. Stop slapping yourself up. Stop disrespecting yourself! Start patting yourself on the back. Start to trust yourself. As you learn how this all works you will GROW IN TRUST AND CONFIDENCE.

You will learn to manifest and MAKE HAPPEN WHAT YOU WANT TO MAKE HAPPEN instead of making the crap happen. You will develop a positive, loving, respectful relationship with you. You will begin to align your conscious desires with your subconscious servo-mechanism. As you do this you entire life will improve.

Those who BELIEVE there is self-sabotage are continuing to perpetuate a limiting belief. It is a lie. Stop believing that. Start believing IN YOUR ABILITY to positively make things happen. Change yourself!

Reverse Engineer From Your Destination To The Beginning

Rejoice! There is a better way. Put an end to the destructive notion of self-sabotage. Transform yourself.

How you begin to do this is to inform and INSTRUCT YOUR SUBCONSCIOUS mind what you do want. "I want to be finan-

cially free." "I want money." "I want good health." "I want love." "I
want great things." "I want to ski well." "I want to prosper and be
successful." Get it? What are the most important words? What
could be the positive feelings associated with each word picture you
send your mind?

Decide what you want that your subconscious mind can begin to go
after. When you express these things in the positive you feel better. It
will get the message because if you THINK POSITIVE
THOUGHTS and FEEL GOOD FEELINGS, it will seek to
deliver these things to you. Get it?

Get in the practice of thinking about, and going for, what you do
want. State your wants in the positive. Learn to speak about what
you do want. Stop talking about what you don't want. Put an end to
focusing on what you don't want. Instead of saying, "I don't want to
be broke." Say "I want to have lots of extra spending money".
'Instead of "I suck" declare "I am magnificent". "I am confident."
"I am powerful!"

Why Doesn't It Change? Because You Are Creating It

Instead of saying, "I don't want a smoker for a mate." Say "I want
someone who is conscious about good health". Get it? Get clear
about what it is you <u>do</u> want. State what you want and what you
want to be!

You feel different when you FOCUS ON WHAT YOU WANT
versus focusing on what you don't want. This makes an incredible
difference! Remember, you get more of what you focus on.

Said another way, what you focus on expands and increases. This is
why you want to REMAIN POSITIVE and feel good. BE POSI-
TIVE and FEEL POSITIVE ABOUT YOURSELF! Get it?

Negative Questions Produce Negative Results

Use what you are learning in this book to CHANGE YOUR MENTAL AND EMOTIONAL STATE from less than glorious to glorious as best you are able to. Whenever you notice you are thinking, saying to yourself or feeling not so good, shift. CHANGE YOURSELF. TAKE CONTROL of your self-talk.

When you positively AFFIRM WHAT YOU WANT, you are learning to do this.

You are putting an end to the negative affirmations you otherwise have used. Please understand, to affirm simply means to declare something to be so. You can affirm something is or that something is not. You can make a positive affirmation such as "I am magnificent" or a negative affirmations such as, "I'm an idiot." Either way your subconscious agrees with your word picture and accompanying feeling. Get it?

Stop negatively affirming and take CONTROL OF YOUR MIND and your life. You are learning how to do this as you read this book. Just be sure you actually do it. Self-talk is a left-brain function. Your primary speech and understanding language centers are in your left hemisphere. So speak nicely to yourself!

Send Your Brain On A Positive Search

Not coincidentally, happiness is a left-brain function. When you feel good and think positively, it is a left-brain function. This may be why many people who have overdeveloped right brains, like artists and creative people are often prone to depression. What we think and say to ourselves matters a great deal.

Yale researchers, in 1987, demonstrated that when a subject was feeling optimistic about life, PET scans of the left hemisphere showed the most activity. The right side of the brain "lit up" when the subjects felt depressed, negative or stressed. Thus, what you say to yourself is critically important. The more POSITIVE AND

HAPPY your self-talk the better you feel. Speak only to bless, heal and prosper yourself. Speak nicely about yourself, and to yourself. Speak nicely of others and all circumstances. Stop creating what you don't want. Create what you do want. Only speak in those terms. Get it?

Speak about what you have, that you enjoy. Reinforce that. Feel good. Feel grateful. Speak about what you want to create that you will enjoy. Reinforce that and feel good about it. Feelings are the key. You want to feel good the majority of your day. You can, too, when you learn how. You can make most of your moments magical and magnificent. The better you feel the easier it becomes to make things happen.

Take Control – Live As A Champion

The better you feel the more better you will feel. It gets easier and it increases. So make it a point to DELIGHT YOURSELF by keeping your mind and feelings positively occupied. When you do you will BEGIN to skyrocket your positive results. You will go from a whiner to a winner. You really can be, do and have anything you want.

How much fun and delight will you make happen today?

"Your life is your spiritual path. It's what's right in front of you. You can't live anyone else's life. The task is to live yours and stop trying to copy one you think looks better."
— *Sandy Nathan*

"All I have is all I need and all I need is all I have in this moment."
— *Byron Katie*

"If you choke your potential before it has an opportunity to become a possibility you will never reach your destiny"
— *Mo Stegall*

"Think of it this way: the input remains the same, so the output has to remain the same. How, then, can you ever create anything new?"
— *Joe Dispenza*

"Always keep an open mind and a compassionate heart."
— *Phil Jackson*

CHAPTER FOUR

Visualization and Feelings Are Key

Your inner thought world is comprised of pictures, sounds and feelings. You MAKE MENTAL IMAGES of memories and future plans. You can fantasize and make things up entirely. You see movies in your head just as you see and hear and feel the world around you. Consciously, you can tell the difference.

You close your eyes and IMAGINE or sense things. You open your eyes and SEE AND SENSE THINGS. You know the difference. Your subconscious mind does not. It doesn't know the difference between a vivid imagined internal image and what it sees on the outside.

It treats your internal images the same as your outer reality. It accepts all of them at face value. That means it accepts as valid your outer experience or inner experience, whichever has the highest signal value.

If You Don't Want To Do It You Will Find An Excuse

We know this from research in sports. Athletes, told to simply visualize improving at a sport, utilized the same muscles and made the same micro muscle movements they would as if they were actually engaged in the activity.

One study, at The University of Chicago by Dr. Biasiotto, divided players into 3 groups: A practice group. They shot free throws. A visualization group, that only imagined throwing free throws. The control group did neither. After 30 days the players were tested again.

Those who practiced demonstrated a 24% improvement. Players who only visualized demonstrated 23% improvement or nearly as much. The group that did neither showed no improvement, as was expected.

What You Say Is What You Get

Another study by Australian Psychologist Alan Richardson demonstrated very similar results. There are a number of other basketball studies, and sports research, whose findings are also similar.

The reason for the improvement in the visualization group is because they always visualized making the shot. They only saw the ball going into the basket. Get it! They imagined success each time they threw the ball in their minds. Visualization adds to skills. It creates our reality.

Researcher, Dr. Richard Suinn at Colorado State University, proved mental rehearsal and visualization actually triggered neuron firings in the muscles. The sequence of neural firings actually created a mental blueprint that facilitates performance in the future.

What You See Is What You Get

His research with skiers hooked up to Electromyographic equipment revealed that skiers who visualized downhill skiing, fired off the electrical impulses in the brain and muscles, producing muscle patterns nearly the same as those skiers used when actually on the hillside.

The Cleveland Clinic Foundation of Ohio discovered that study participants who only visualized doing bicep curls increased their strength by 13.5%. They had increases in strength and they only visualized! No exercise. Still, they experienced gains because they used their minds.

These subjects visualized five times a week for fourteen days. They did no other exercise. Had they lifted the weights they would have made larger gains but this study shows that visualization adds to performance. It demonstrates the mind accepts it as real. Visualization works and it is always working.

Thoughts Become Things – What You Focus On Expands

Do you get it? Mental practice, rehearsal, visualization, and imagination using all five senses can prepare you for success and help you get much closer in life to where you want to be. Computer specialist, Natan Sharansky, spent nine years in solitary confinement in a USSR prison.

He played mental chess all the while. He decided he might as well use his time as an opportunity to 'become the chess champion of the world'. In fact, he did. In 1996 Sharansky beat Garry Kasparov, then the reigning world chess champion.

Celebrity visualizers: Billie Jean King, tennis champ, Muhammad Ali, boxing champ, Conor McGregor, UFC champion, Arnold Schwarzenegger, bodybuilder, politician, movie star, Jay Z, rapper, record producer, Lindsey Vonn, pro skier, Oprah Winfrey, billionaire TV personality. Actors Jim Carrey, Will Smith, Denzel Washington.

Carli Lloyd, World Cup champion, Kerri Walsh and Misty May-Treanor, the most successful beach volleyball duo, Tyler Perry, actor, director songwriter, Lady GaGa singer, entertainer. Tiger Woods, golf pro. Successful people use their minds on purpose for success. They use it deliberately.

If You See It In Your Head You Can Hold It In Your Hand

I could go on and on listing all of those professional athletes, celebrities and others who use affirmations and visualizations to program their mind and future successes. One example is professional golfer Jack Nicklaus who said this about his use of visualization, "I never hit a shot, not even in practice, without having a very sharp, in-focus picture of it in my head."

Remember brain research, as mentioned in the skiing studies, demonstrates visualization as utilizing the same internal neural firing and pathways that physical actions do. It is confirmed.

It affects your attention, perception, planning, memory, and motor control. When you visualize you are rehearsing, preparing, training and conditioning yourself for performance in the real world. Mental rehearsal is the same as actual rehearsal. It can't replace years of experience but it <u>can</u> OPTIMIZE EVERYTHING YOU DO.

Dare To Dream Big - Make Your Dreams Come True

Mental rehearsal increases performance. It helps increase confidence, because as you improve your confidence improves. Winning more means more winning. It increases states of motivation and flow. You get better because you IMAGINE YOURSELF GETTING BETTER.

Mental rehearsal is most effective when it includes all of the senses. If you can imagine, seeing, hearing, tasting, smelling and feeling while you visualize it is most powerful. Some people get hung up on this. They claim they can't see their pictures. The fact is they respond to the internal imagery but the pictures are outside of their awareness.

"The brain has infinite capacity. The more you put into it the more it will hold. The human brain grows the way biceps do. Every time we use visualization, the ability to visualize expands," said Glen Dowman, founder of The Institutes For The Achievement of Human Potential.

See It - Feel It - Hear It - Speak It - Taste It - Smell It - Be It

Anyone can learn to visualize better. The way you currently visualize is how you learned to visualize. Your visualization muscle was conditioned along certain lines. If you want to improve it, do it repeatedly.

The way you USE YOUR BRAIN is how you were conditioned. As with other changes of thought, feeling and behavior you can improve your ability to SEE INTERNAL IMAGES through practice.

Still, you can get incredible results just by sensing or feeling what you otherwise would be seeing! If this weren't POSSIBLE blind people could never GET their GOALS. So you don't have to visualize well, to make things happen. The most important aspect of visualization is the feeling you generate while visualizing. It is the emotions that make the difference! I'll share more about this in a bit.

Be Willing To Ask – Be Willing To Explore

This is a good time to introduce you to my friend, two-time World Class Olympian High Jumper, actor and writer Jamie Nieto. As an actor he portrayed Roberto Clemente in 'Baseball's Last Hero: The Roberto Clemente Story.' He competed in the Olympics in 2004 and 2012 and numerous other games.

Jamie was injured in April of 2016 while performing a backflip. Something he has executed thousands of times. He slipped, landed on his head and became paralyzed. He was put on a ventilator to help him breathe and placed in intensive care. He could only flinch his left pectoral muscle a bit.

The prognosis was grim. He underwent surgery. He did not sever his spinal cord so there was some hope he would regain limited movement. That did not deter Jamie. He kept his faith and determination to recover.

The Quality Of Life Is Determined By The Quality Of Questions

As of this writing Jamie is progressing. He is up walking and using his hands and arms. His right foot improved somewhat, first. His left foot was lagging behind. He said, "it got frustrating because my body wouldn't do what I wanted it to do. Then I thought I am not going to let my body win."

"You can't beat me!" It started to turn around. "My feet started moving. I started taking steps. It let me know that I would walk again and I am going to run again! I still have the fight of an

Olympian. I AM BETTER than this and I am going to keep fighting." His attitude is incredible. His faith is strong!

He says. "One day you are floating along and your life is going well and everything is cool." Two weeks prior to the accident he shared on his Facebook wall that he was happy and was working a lot, writing for television.

End Chronic Negative Thinking

"Then maybe you get in a car accident, or you are doing a training thing and you flip and hit your head. You never know what can happen. You have to take advantage of your time and your life and enjoy it."

"EMBRACE YOUR LOVED ONES and do the best. BE THE BEST PERSON YOU CAN BE to everyone you meet. You may not like everybody but that is okay. Just be the best person you can be. Seeing the overwhelming response to my injury from people really let me know how many people's lives I have touched. I AM BLESSED."

"I thank God for all their prayers and support. I am going to try to document this thing from now until I am 100% better with no complications. I will keep you guys posted. I love you all and I thank God for you all and how blessed I am."

Asking The Right Questions Is A Skill For Life

He has a vision for his total recovery. His attitude and how he uses his mind is the foundation for the changes he is making. He walks, using a walker, each step a deliberate conscious effort. His doctors are amazed at the speed of his recovery.

He says, "I am moving a lot better. I am figuring things out. It has been a tough experience. It's not easy, relearning how to use my arms and walk again. I'm moving my hands and feet again. I am getting stronger so it is getting better."

I knew, if anyone can accomplish this it is Jamie. His training as an athlete conditioned him to use his mind and his will to determine to walk again. Jamie realizes this too. That and his faith made it possible.

Attitude Is Everything

He is making incredible progress and is surprising everyone. He still has a way to go but he is closing in on it daily. He is a remarkable man and a wonderful friend.

Jamie also had a big goal. He had a dream. He had a vision. He imagined himself walking, unassisted, down the aisle with his bride on their wedding day. This was a tremendous challenge. Would he? Could he?

Yes, he made his dream come true on Saturday, July 22, 2017, fifteen months after being told he might never walk again. The event received a lot of media coverage. However, for Jamie, the best part is accomplishing what he set out to do. He got to celebrate in a number of ways on his wedding day.

Use Questions Anytime Anywhere For Anything

You may never be challenged as he or others are in life or you may have been equally or challenged in even worse ways. Still, you can USE VISUALIZATION to help you GET WHAT YOU WANT. From Jamie's example and the numerous studies into this area we know visualization is a much needed and useful skill. It works. If you regularly and consistently apply it, you can excel and make major changes!

It benefits all who learn to harness it. The bad news is you are already visualizing whether you are aware of it or not. You are already using your brain to bring the negative things into your life that you do not want.

Your brain transports you. You are the passenger. You may be taken on rides to places you don't want to go. Your mind just runs on and on. It does its own thing and you keep getting what you don't want.

The good news is you can take control and learn to harness it. You can put its positive power to work for you. You can use it to make incredible changes and improvements. You can get some really impressive results. You can truly be, do and have anything you want when you use your mind correctly.

The principle operating here is, since the subconscious doesn't know, your visualization it isn't real, it has to act on it. It gets the message through repetition and your strong emotions. The stronger the clearer!

Visualize To Breakthrough: You Can Pretend Anything And Master It - The Agoraphobic

One day I received a call from a woman who told me that she had not left her home in for many years. She'd seen all the top therapists and top change agents, spent loads of money, but none were able to help her. She wanted my help. I said I wouldn't let her hire me to help her. She was shocked and dismayed.

She asked why and I said, 'because I don't want to be on your top list of failures. What I do works so I refuse to be put on a list like that. If I'm going to help you it has to work. We have to succeed so I'm not going to take any money.' Once she got the results she wanted, then, she could pay me.

I did want to protect myself, and my reputation. This way she couldn't say I was one of the many people she had hired to try and help her. I wasn't about to go down that road with all the other doctors, therapists, hypnotists whom she named. It also set me apart as someone who got results and was certain he could help.

I Never Met A Strong Person With An Easy Past

I asked what she would most like to do. She told me she would like to take a drive to a favorite shopping place. It was a lovely drive. She'd like to able to shop and spend time and hang out outdoors and enjoy the world. I asked her when the last time she had done that. She told me it had been 11 years. Can you imagine being confined to your house, indoors, for eleven years? But that is what it was.

I asked her to go back and remember a time that she made that drive and enjoyed it. I asked her what she saw along the way, what she heard and how she felt. I wanted her to go behind the wheel in her mind and make the drive feeling wonderful. She did.

There were many lovely sites and a large bridge she drove over on her way to this favorite spot of hers. I had her imagine it from her point of view and feel all the wonderful sensations of seeing each landmark she passed. I had her recall the positive thoughts and internal things she said to herself, as well as what she could hear outside. She got to where she wanted to go, all in her head, and we ran through the entire scenario a handful of times. Each time she felt better and better. She was thrilled with these memories.

First Learn Stand Then Learn Fly - Wax On Wax Off

Then I told her that was enough for today and to call back two days later. A couple days later she called me and we repeated that process numerous times. Then, I said, 'That's great, call me back in a couple days.' She did that again we went through the process.

I began adding a few other things she would like to see and do - memories of places, and had her travel there too. Each time she called she'd take these mental trips of where she really wanted to go to again. I'd drop hints such as, 'Wouldn't it be cool if you were able to someday get in your car, as you had in the past, and drive to wherever you wanted to go most?' I didn't make a big deal of it.

Of course, she'd respond with, 'Yeah it would be wonderful!' I'd say 'Okay, let's go back and run it in your head again.' We did this every other day for about the span of 10 or 12 days. Maybe an hour, (usually much shorter) at most each time, except for the very first call, which was longer.

Winners Never Quit – Quitters Never Win – Which Are You

The weekend was coming up and I said 'OK, I will talk to you next week. I want you to surprise yourself and let me know when you talk to me.' She called me before the weekend ended and said, 'You'll never guess what!'

'I got in the car. I drove over the bridge. I went to the mall. I shopped. I went to the park and spent time outdoors. I did everything I wanted! Thank you, Thank you!' I said, 'That is great but you did it. You took the steps. Congratulate yourself!'

I said, 'I bet there are many other things you want to do. This was only the start. Imagine being able to do anything safely that you want to do.' She used her mind to move from being shut indoors for nearly 12 years to being able to go outside and live life.

The Struggles Today Develops Your Strength For Tomorrow

From that point on I began receiving gift after gift. I got gold jewelry. I got desserts. I got all sorts of wonderful gifts. Almost every week something arrived in the mail. I got paid. She was so grateful. I told her the gifts were unnecessary but I received gifts for a number of years.

I have since lost touch. The point is she made major changes in her mind first seeing what it was she wanted to be able to accomplish. She repeated it safely and comfortably, the desire growing in her, to actually do it in outer life. She did. That huge step meant she could do anything she put her mind to.

It was evidence of winning! If she succeeded with this, she would succeed with anything. She was happier and healthier as a result. Mindset matters. It had kept her trapped. She had a habit of being a shut-in. Once she broke those habits she was free to create new ones to do what she wanted to enjoy her life.

Use Questions Anytime Anywhere For Anything

Whatever occupies your mind, your thoughts, what you say to yourself and your feelings, good or bad, is what you get more of. It is what you create for yourself. It is that which you will experience.

The stronger your feelings the more supercharged your visualization is. This means if you are focused on crap you can get some really impressive, crappy results. But if you FOCUS ON GOOD THINGS, and feeling positive you can GET some wonderfully Positive and Powerful Results.

Get it? It is always up to you! It is always up to how you use your brain. You determine the quality of the life you live by the thoughts you think. Stop using it haphazardly for less than glorious results. Stop that now! Start learning to use visualization and your brain to get what you want instead. Use it with purpose!

Keep The Positive Direction In Mind

You can powerfully PROGRAM YOUR MIND, by visualizing and affirming what you want a number of times, each day. The stronger your positive feelings are, the quicker and easier your subconscious gets the message. Now, I am going to share with you the secret sauce.

Think about what you want as if you already have it. Instead of affirming "I want a new car" say, "I love my brand new wonderful car." "I have my fabulous dream car and I love it!" The make and model is up to you. As you do this feel the incredible feelings you'd have if you just got this brand new car.

Do this repeatedly with the object of your desire. Whatever positive, good thing you want, it doesn't have to be a car. Remember, repetition and emotion. Do it over and over again. You become, or you get, what you think about most of the time. <u>You</u> fulfill your obsessions!

Know What You Want And Go For It

"I have more than enough money." "My business is prosperous." "I am financially free." "I live abundantly." "I am healthy." "I have tremendous health and wellbeing." "I am physically fit." "I enjoy my loving relationship." "I adore my incredible home." "I love the feeling of skiing safely down the mountainside." "I love the snow, the breeze in my hair, the spectacular view." "This is the good life."

Get it? Declare it. Affirm it. Speak it over and over inside <u>and</u> out loud with GREAT ENTHUSIASM! Feel strong, wonderful, positive emotion. Spend most of your day thinking positive on what you have. See it in your mental movie theater. "I am" "I have" Declare it! FEEL IT! FEEL GOOD about it!

Direct Your Mind Towards What You Want To Include

Another thing you must know about your subconscious mind is it is eternally present. It doesn't know past or future. You consciously do, it doesn't. I mean, think about how weird your dreams can be. Your subconscious mind thinks present. If you want something that is off in the future it has no way of understanding that, so it remains in the future. "I want this." Your subconscious mind thinks "Yes I do."

It say "Yes I want this" and so you keep wanting it. If you think, "I am this, I am doing this, I am having this right now", your subconscious mind gets it. When <u>it</u> gets it, <u>then</u> you can. It will put into operation all of your subconscious resources to help you make it happen. That is what the RAS does for you, Remember? It looks to create matches between what you believe and the outer world.

So when you visualize IMAGINE YOUR DREAM, your goal, your desire as if they already have come true. Feel what it feels like to live with them, right now. They are yours, now, in your present. Even though outer circumstances may not have yet caught up with your inner reality. Claim them. Own them!

Stop Comparing Stop Wondering

<u>This</u> is how you reprogram your subconscious mind. You tell it, show it, and FEEL ALL THE GOOD things you want, 'as if' you already have them. You show it, tell it, and FEEL IT again and again until you do in the outer world. From the inner to the outer is how this all works. It goes from an idea to the tangible.

Yes, it requires some time. It takes time to exercise, and condition your body. It takes time to prepare, cook, serve, and enjoy a meal. It takes time to get from one end of the country to the other. It takes time to plant a seed and harvest. Everything takes some time! Get over it!

You want magic and want it overnight but that isn't how it works. You weren't a baby and then a fully-grown adult. Everything is a process. You condition your subconscious mind for success. <u>You</u> condition it. You <u>condition</u> it. You condition <u>it</u>! Do you understand, yet? Do it and YOU WILL GET THE RESULTS, <u>but</u> only if you do it!

The only thing that cannot be done is this. No one else can do it for you! <u>You</u> must do it. You must focus on what you want and ignore the contrast of present circumstances not matching your inner reality, yet. They will CHANGE IN TIME with the new thoughts, but it will take time for outer circumstances to catch up. Focus on the positive and exclude the rest. Concentrate. Stay focused and keep the faith!

It Is Your Decision And No One Else's

Exercise: Pick one thing. One goal. Create a mantra or affirmation around it. If necessary, go back to the examples I gave you previously. Focus on one. See it inside, visualize (or sense it) and feel it. Chant your mantra day and night with passion and enthusiasm. Keep going until you get it. Be patient. Consider doing it most of the time for 30, 60 or 90 days, repeatedly. Do it longer, if necessary. Go for it!

Exercise: Get a photograph of something you strongly want. It could be a picture of a car, a new home, a watch, something you truly desire. Sit with it on your lap, or in front of you. Don't move, remain as still as you can. Look at the photo and trace it with your eyes. Look and memorize every detail you can. Look at it. See every bit of it. Examine it for five minutes.

Close your eyes. For another five minutes recreate the photo in your mind. See it as vividly as you can. Imagine it fully. See every detail you remember. Set a timer for each session of five minutes. Do this daily. Your ability to visualize what you want will grow. If you DO THIS DAILY you will be surprised.

Here is an added benefit. Use the photograph of something you already strongly want. Remember and feel all the good feelings too. When the exercise is over take another couple minutes and see it, feel what it is like to have it now. Imagine it already yours. Affirm having it. Then, let go, and go about your day.

Exercise Takes Time – Champions Aren't Made In A Day

You can do this any number of times during your day, and especially upon arising and before going to bed. Many positive changes will occur for you as you progress. Stick with it to discover what these are.

Exercise: Write down what you want. Use the previous affirmation examples as a guide. "I have a loving partner". "I make an extra

$1000 dollars per month." "I live in my dream home." Once you have an important dream goal statement, close your eyes and relax.

We are going to use your imagination. It doesn't matter whether you see it vividly or if you have a sense of it. However you imagine is fine. The important thing is you spend time deliberately doing this.

No Whining Stop Worrying

SEE IT as if it is yours RIGHT NOW. FEEL THE WONDERFUL FEELINGS you would have right now, if you already had it. Imagine you have your desire already. IMAGINE HOW GOOD IT FEELS.

For example: Imagine, you already live in your dream home. What does that feel like? What did it feel like when you got it? You don't have to know how you got your goal, just imagine that you did, ALREADY. Feel the sensations. Make them as strong as you can. If they are subtle at first, increase them.

Imagine the home fully. How does it look outside? Imagine the landscape. Where do you park? What's the yard like? What is the interior like? How many rooms? Which is your favorite? How is it decorated? Where do you spend most of your time? How does all of this make you feel? Who is living with you? GET IT? Walk through the house. Sit in your favorite room and enjoy. Imagine entertaining there.

Who Is In Charge

Create it as fully as you are able. Whether you picture it or sense it, what is most important, are the wonderful feelings of already having it, right now. This is your home! This fabulous home is yours.

Savor these moments! You can repeat this any time. I encourage you to do it frequently, feeling it fully.

Imagine it as if it already has happened. Imagining what you want, as if you already have it, IS the most powerful way you can program yourself to get it. Your mind sees you with it and feels what it is like for you to have the good you desire.

Another way is to consider the when you want to get. Someday? Anytime? When, in the future? What is the date? So if you prefer you can set a deadline. That is fine. That gives you a target to work towards. That can work. I discuss more about this later. There are some pro and cons. You should know them.

Make Your Dreams Come True

The best and most efficient way to get your desires is to assert, affirm and declare them in the present. It is all right now and it feels glorious. This instructs your subconscious mind what you want. It tells it precisely. Think, "I am rich." "I have plenty of money." "I feel great." YOU HAVE EVERYTHING WITHIN.

YOU are these already. You have an INCREDIBLE ally in your subconscious. It knows what to do and how to do it. Use good judgment and tell it the positive, productive WONDERFUL things you want it to do so you can begin getting those results. Be patient. Persist. Never quit. Tough times may come, they usually do.

Push through them. Persist to get your goal. LOVE YOURSELF, forgive yourself, trust yourself and keep going. It may take some time reconditioning your mental muscle to give you what you want, but it will 'get the picture' soon. You PROGRAM YOUR MIND while you take action steps. I'll share more about this shortly.

Keep It In Mind: Everything Is A Process – We Are In Process

Your subconscious will GET IT QUICKER if you pick one thing to focus on exclusively. Once you make that happen move on to the next thing. It gets easier as you practice it. You will re-educate your subconscious mind in this manner. It already says "yes' to you whether you are thinking positive or negative thoughts. Remember this! Keep this in mind! Give it great things to SAY YES about.

Be grateful you have such a magnificent servant at your disposal. It is faithful and reliable. It is your BEST FRIEND. Treat it well. Program it with what **YOU WANT** it to do. YOU CAN do this. If anyone in the world can do this, and many have, you can do this! Do it today!

CHAPTER FIVE

The Basis Of Your Pain

We tend to like things the same. We get used to it. We expect there to be consistency in others and events. We want it. This is quite normal. It's all part of being human. What about when things are different?

What happens inside us? What do you see or visualize in your mind when a loved one is uncharacteristically late? You expected the person at a certain time and place. Yet, you haven't heard from them. Do you have a change in self-talk as well? What do you begin to say to yourself?

Is it positive or negative? We either feel good or not so good based on what we expect, or imagine to be the case. In the loved one example, if they show up late, we may be relieved. Why relieved?

What You See Is What You Get

Because many people, faced with unexpected events, tend to begin to imagine what possibly went wrong. This is because our brain is predisposed to do this. It alerts us to what is wrong so we might fix it.

Remember, our brain works to keep us alive and to keep us the same. While it could IMAGINE WONDERFUL POSSIBILITIES, it mostly does not. Unless you take control of it, it runs countless negative scenarios each worse than the one before. However, once trained, it can run positive wonderful scenarios.

Negative emotions get triggered. Our self-talk accelerates and gets worse. We begin to get worried, frustrated, angry even fearful. We are doing all of this to ourselves because our brain is the driver. We are going along for a nightmare ride. Then suddenly the person arrives.

When The Going Gets Tough The Tough Get Going

We may be relieved none of the terrible things we imagined happened, but we are angry! We might even read them the riot act for putting us through what we went through. We blame them for our internal self-talk and negative images. They may be genuinely surprised by our reaction saying "RELAX!!!"

They could get angry too. Feeding off of your negative feelings and what you say, they could get mad right back at you. Then instead of a pleasant meeting both parties are disturbed. Has this ever happened to you? It sure has to me. It will continue to happen until we take charge and learn how to change it.

You will DISCOVER how to make many changes as you continue to study and APPLY THIS MATERIAL. One thing you can begin doing, if you don't already do this, is to acknowledge the runaway thoughts as they begin. As soon as you become aware of your negative, less than glorious pictures, self-talk and feelings, acknowledge them by saying, "thanks for sharing." This serves to take the sting and resistance out of it. It can prevent your emotions from flooding.

We Are Powerful Creators And The Results We Get We Created

Consider this. You're standing right next to and in front of the bumper of a parked car on a steep incline. The brakes give out and it begins to roll. You can put your hand out, or stand there, and stop it. You can do this because there is no momentum built up. You caught it early enough. You couldn't if you were 20 feet below. You'd have to jump out of the way. Gravity starts the car rolling. Momentum picks up and you wouldn't be able to stop it. The same applies here. Catch it early enough and you can prevent it from getting worse. So, thank it for sharing. It takes the sting out of it. It interrupts it. You stop the raging.

You aren't mad at yourself. You're not screaming 'sabotage'. You realize your tendency to engage your mind this way but you become aware. You notice the negativity beginning and you say, "Thanks for sharing". You can add, "but no thanks" if you wish. You can say, "Cancel". I have used both.

When you say, "Thanks for sharing," you aren't preventing or damming up the flow of negativity, rather you are allowing it. You are diverting it. Get it? You aren't trying to stuff it back inside. That rarely or never works. When you stuff it, it tries all the harder to get back out. It comes at you more vigorously.

Everyone Faces Challenges

Diverting works well for this reason. If you have ever tried to resist thinking about something, you know how difficult that is. That's the problem with stuffing. This works because you don't stuff it. You simply acknowledge and THANK YOURSELF for wanting to share something. This can work wonders.

Never create more problems by fighting with yourself. Blaming yourself only creates more negative issues. Stop that. Simply, notice, acknowledge, validate and move on. "Thanks for sharing, but no thanks". Yes, you may have to do it more than once. Do it as much or as little as you need to, to move on.

Going back to the loved one being late example, something changed in us because we are used to things being a certain way. We expected something. As a result our inner mechanism went automatic. That's what all of this is. Automatic thoughts, feelings and behaviors create pain.

Exercise Takes Time – Champions Aren't Made In A Day

We change negative ones for ones that bring us relief, or enjoyment or happiness or better. Get it? We replace ones that don't serve us with those that do. That is the art and science to my methods.

We believe things about ourselves and about others, events and the world. We tend to see things not as they are but as we imagine them to be. When they aren't as we are used to, extra activity begins inside us.

Something changes out of the ordinary. What happens within? How do you react? You react out of habit. You find yourself traveling chronic old ways of behavior and negative self-talk. You end up feeling worse and worse. Right? Well? Think about it. Take your time. Wouldn't it be wonderful to change that?

Godxilla Changed

Chris 'Godxilla' Taylor grew up in Milwaukee. As a black youth he experienced much hardship and the opportunities around him were limited. Violence and drugs were pervasive. The economy was tanking. He sought a way out through religion. That didn't work for him. He felt oppressed by government policies. He was a hustler and lived the 'street life' but refused to commit serious crimes. The social pressures were the hardest things he had to maneuver through in the ghetto.

He didn't want a 9-5 job. So he made rap records. He did okay in 'Gangsta Rap' and toured the country with acts he produced. However, the success he wanted was elusive. Many around him were getting incarcerated. Chris knew the 'street life' was a no-winner. He wanted better!

He believed he had to get away. Chris knew he had to seek better opportunities. He moved to Los Angeles to pursue the music business and decided to go to school at 34. His reward was a degree in sound engineering. This opened new doors. He became an instructor at the school and worked his way up to become an associate dean and campus director.

You Already Affirm Your Experience – Good Or Bad

Chris had a MAJOR SHIFT in his thinking, from street life to education. He reformed himself and began a new life. He became a family man. He discovered he didn't need the glitz and that money wouldn't buy him happiness.

Chris says; "I am happy. I am living life on my own terms. I am high off of the challenge, not some drug or some power trip. No matter if I actually ended up homeless again, I won't return to drugs or criminality again. I won't fall for those traps and because of that I will always have a fighting chance."

He found that materialism was not redeeming. His spirit was. He found A NEW WAY, because he wanted it. Chris says: "When you grow past the hood there's no limit to where you can land".

What expectations do you live from? Think about it, really. Yes, we expect sunrise, start there. Take a moment and reflect on these questions. You may even write down your answers if you prefer.

Your Thoughts Shape Your Results And Your Reality

Exercise: What do you expect to happen each day? What do you expect of yourself, of loved ones, friends, strangers, and the barista? Remember, my example of a loved one showing up late? What do you expect or yourself and others? What do you expect of circumstances and events? What do you expect of other drivers on the road? Get it? Consider any situation you can, one at a time.

See if you can discover how sometimes you create your own pain because of your expectations. Sometimes, you CREATE YOUR OWN JOY. How do you do that? Explore. Discover.

Expectation is another word for beliefs. What do you believe should happen? What do you believe is the right thing? What do you believe about these people and events? What do you believe should be the case? This is powerful when done on driving. We have so many rules and expectations. We react quickly and sometimes explosively. Before you know it you may be swearing and giving the finger. Get it? Explore!

Skill Comes From Doing

What are your rules? How should things be? How should people treat you? How should you treat others? Realize a belief, an expectation and a rule follows the word 'should'. Be alert anytime you hear yourself thinking or saying it. Where did you get these rules and beliefs? Can you recall a time or experience? Whose rules were they before you adopted them as your own? Can you remember? Be open, honest and willing!

What did you discover doing this exercise? Did you uncover some of you rules, beliefs and expectations about yourself, others and the world? I invite you to keep exploring. Pick other areas to explore. There are many different places in your life where you will benefit from uncovering your rules, beliefs and expectations.

Do you think this is a worthwhile exercise? Why? Why not? Did you do it? Why or why not? Will you do it? Who knows? You may notice or learn something you were not aware of. Then what? Will that be good or not so good? Figure it out. Spend some time with this. I mean, really, the payoff can be huge.

What You Think About You Bring About

Get to know yourself and what you believe and expect. This is important. Realize, the answer to the question "why did you do it" or "why didn't you do it" will reveal more of the beliefs you hold. Are you getting this?

Many people think seeing is believing. They think if they see it, they will BECOME CONVINCED of it. The opposite is true when you manifest and make things happen. Believing is seeing. Only after you believe do you actually see. It is how the brain works. This is why what you believe is important.

Do you BELIEVE YOU CAN? Is it possible? Do YOU DESERVE IT? We will come back to beliefs many times in this book. Beliefs are very important. Numerous studies demonstrate why. Take the placebo effect for example. A placebo is an ingredient, or object, that has no known power or effect. It is considered inert. The placebo isn't important. The placebo <u>effect</u> is!

When a person believes something may be good for them, their attitude toward treatment, as I mentioned before, has an increased likelihood to benefit them. Get it? This is why it's important to examine and change limiting beliefs to supportive ones. It's their attitude and their beliefs that make a difference. People can get better whether or not there is any actual benefit to the drug, treatment or object.

Exploration Is The Doorway To Adventure

This <u>is</u> the placebo effect. Every single medicine, prescription or not, valid or not, is effective <u>due</u> to the placebo effect. This is because the placebo effect is <u>always</u> in operation. It is always in operation, anytime a person takes a drug or medication, or has an expectation toward an outcome, medical or otherwise. A person can believe in luck, amulets, or a ritual like spitting or combing one's hair. It is always a part of it.

Unless, it's not. Then it is called the Nocebo Effect. Even then it is working, but in the reverse. The beliefs, the expectations, the placebo effect is always ongoing. Just as there are positive and negative beliefs there are the placebo and nocebo effects. The Nocebo effect means if you don't think anything will help you, then, most likely, it won't. So, it could be the person doesn't believe anything will help, so it doesn't.

The most extreme example of the nocebo effect is voodoo deaths. A person believes they are cursed and will die, and sadly they do. This has been documented. Still, negative thoughts and beliefs affect each of us. They affect our health and wellbeing. This is reason enough to examine our beliefs and then choose to create positive and beneficial ones. The placebo and nocebo effects are all about beliefs.

Here are some the fascinating statistics regarding the placebo. Dr. Becher of Harvard University, researched pain and placebo. He found morphine worked in 52% of the cases. The placebo worked in 40% of the cases. Thus the placebo was 75% as effective as morphine. Imagine that! The placebo works three quarters of the time. That is incredibly powerful for something that "shouldn't work and isn't real". Get it?

Become Powerful

In many cases it is alleged the placebo works better than the medicine, because the medicine may include toxic ingredients. What we believe is what is important. Our beliefs either support us or they do not.

Pay attention to this following true story. "Mr. Wright," was diagnosed as having cancer in 1957. He was given only days to live. He was hospitalized in Long Beach, California, with orange sized tumors. He learned scientists had discovered a horse serum that appeared to be effective in fighting cancer. He begged his doctor to treat him with the drug called Krebiozen.

Dr. Philip West, agreed and gave Mr. Wright his first injection on a Friday afternoon. The following Monday, the doctor found his patient up and out of his "deathbed." He was upbeat and joking with the nurses. The doctor's notes included this statement. The tumors "had melted like snowballs on a hot stove." Mr. Wright was fine for some time thereafter.

Be Receptive And Expect Good Things

However, a couple of months later, Wright read some medical reports that the horse serum was considered bogus. It was not effective. It was a quack remedy. He suffered relapse immediately. Dr. West told him not to believe what you read in the papers. He gave him a new injection.

He said this medicine was "a new super-refined double strength" version of the Krebiozen. Actually, it was only water, a placebo, but again, the tumors melted. For another two months Mr. Wright was again the picture of good health. That is, until he read a report stating that Krebiozen was definitely worthless. Sadly, he died two days later.

You Have To Get Over Your Own Previous Conditioning

Isn't that an AMAZING story? Doctors often dismiss the case of Mr. Wright as a strange tale medicine cannot explain. Almost none are trained to understand that a patient's beliefs can make disease go away.

I had a magnetic bracelet my mother gave me. It was for pain. I didn't know if it worked or not. I was willing to wear it. I didn't know if I believed it would work or not. I had a physician ask me about it and I told him it was a magnetic bracelet for pain. He dismissed it in a huff, stating, "It's only a placebo!"

Silly medical practitioner! He should have known better. He could have been dismissing, not only me, but my belief in something positive and beneficial. On the other hand, another doctor asked, and when I told him, he exclaimed. "Cool, tell me how it works!" What an amazing difference in attitude from two medical practitioners. Still, unfortunately, there are some who dismiss it. I want a doctor who doesn't.

Most scientists now know the placebo effect is more powerful than anyone had been able to demonstrate in past years. The power of this belief can border on the miraculous. Currently, some researchers are using new approaches to brain imagery and uncovering numerous biological mechanisms inside us that can turn a thought, a belief or a desire into A POWERFUL CHANGE agent affecting the body.

Stop Fighting What You Don't Want

Researchers have learned and are beginning to seriously understand that a great deal of human perception isn't based on information flowing into the brain from the outer world, but what goes on inside the brain, based on previous experience, beliefs and expectations as to what happens next. They know believing is seeing.

Studies have demonstrated that placebos can work like the "real drugs" they replace. Placebos can affect changes in pulse rate, blood pressure, gastric functions, electrical skin resistance, itching and skin conditions. They can cause side effects like nausea and diarrhea.

The placebo effect is so powerful and pervasive that many doctors critical of 'natural cures' and alternative methods blame their effectiveness on the placebo effect. Isn't that sad? Aren't placebos and the way our minds work fascinating? The powers of our mind are incredible!

Author, Marilyn Sanger, criticized me, in one of her books in the early 1990's for stating my work is to help people consciously engineer the placebo effect. We may not be able to do everything by belief alone, but we should at least do everything we can. Let's face it. What we believe either supports who we are, and what we are doing, or it does not.

The Way You Tame Negativity Is To Replace It With Positivity

For now, begin the exploration into your own beliefs. Do the exercise before you continue reading. Explore your beliefs. What do you believe about any topic? We have beliefs about god, the universe, the government, our abilities, money, romance, eating, hobbies, the media and more. There is no shortage of what we believe.

FEEL FREE to write down as many of these beliefs you can discover. Then begin to decide whether or not you want to keep them or if you would prefer to change some of them. Consider what you would want to believe instead. Sometimes it is simply the opposite. The old belief is, "I am a failure" and you want to believe the new belief, "I am a success." Notice that many beliefs follow our, "I am" statements.

You can easily recognize them. Whenever you say, "I am" determine what the reason, or the because, is that follows the "I am." What is the reason you are it? "I am late because... I am broke because... I am lonely because..." Examine these statements that follow and determine what you would prefer to believe instead. Write these limiting beliefs out and the beliefs you would rather believe.

Repeat this process to determine what that says or means about you. Answer the question, what does, thinking, feeling or doing that mean about you? 'and that means X about me?' What does it mean that you're late, broke or lonely? "I'm late and that means I'm ... (you might say) "... it means I am careless, or thoughtless, or preoccupied, or a bad person." Get it? "I'm broke and that means I ... don't know how to save money" or 'It means I'm careless about money." What is your judgement or belief about you? Examine your belief statements and determine what you'd prefer to believe. Write out your preferred beliefs. Let go of what does not support you and what you don't want to believe and affirm, repeat and rehearse what you do want to believe that supports you.

There is more to come...

Remember to FOCUS ON WHAT YOU WANT as though you already have it. This means believing you have it on the inside, before it shows up in your outer reality.

Shift From Negative Feelings To Powerful Positive Ones

Whether you actually do the exercises or not, and I hope you do, however, you spend your time I hope it will be marvelous!

"Our beliefs control our bodies, our minds and thus our lives."
—— *Bruce Lipton*

"Great work is done by people who are not afraid to be great."
—— *Fernando Flores*

CHAPTER SIX

Change Limitations Into Opportunities

Why do people opt for the less than glorious? Why do they maintain their problems and limitations? Why do they make changing hard work that requires effort? Have you ever thought about this?

One of the reasons is that people adopt notions, beliefs, frames of minds and attitude that include concepts such as, "Without pain there is no gain." Or "It isn't real or worth it unless you work really hard and suffer." Or "Happiness is being unrealistic," OR "You can't be happy all the time."

There may be many reasons or excuses why someone opts to feel bad instead of feeling good. They may not THINK IT IS POSSIBLE or that they deserve it. You, of course, now recognize these as belief statements, right? What if you could be happy all the time? What if happiness is a choice you make?

Success Is An Attitude, A Mindset, A Decision, A Commitment

People put all sorts of conditions and requirements on life. They may have an unrealistic view of what it means to BE HAPPY or to be a positive thinker. I could go on and on I'm sure. If you are a person who embraces some these beliefs you might wish to consider them as things you assume are true, but which may not actually be true.

It's a bit tricky. People defend their beliefs very strongly. They don't want to believe that they may not be true. We think our beliefs are true and our reasons valid. We cling to them. We insist we know what's best and what's right. We feel as if we have a monopoly on the truth. Many of us certainly act as if we do.

We don't have a monopoly, BUT we think we do. We'll argue our case, our point of view, vehemently to prove others wrong and ourselves as correct. We have numerous times, haven't we? We defend our beliefs even if they are ridiculous. I sure have, haven't you? It's how we grew up and how we were conditioned.

We just hate to be wrong about things. In order to begin to be free and move more freely into a new way of being, we have to be willing to allow some room for anything else to be possible. We need to be willing to explore some other options, even just a little bit. Could you choose happiness most of the time?

You Can Have Anything If You Give Up The Belief You Can't

Before you get into bed at night you remove your clothing. Perhaps, you put on other bed clothes that are more comfortable. Still, you change. You remove your clothes. Stop for a moment and consider all of your beliefs as articles of clothing. Use your imagination. Do this now.

Imagine! You can remove your beliefs in the same way. Take them off, fold them up, or hang them up on a rack. Once you divest yourself of your old beliefs in this manner you may be willing to try on some other new beliefs for a time being. Yours are still there where you left them. Don't worry. You can always get them back whenever you wish, if you must.

Relax, they are right there! What is the worst that would happen if you tried on other beliefs? Really, what is the worst thing that could happen if you believed you could always BE HAPPY? What if you believed happiness is a choice you can make? What if you make it?

Imagine believing differently for just a little while. What if you could entertain the opposite of limiting beliefs? What if you imagined you can find love, be successful, and have all the money you desire? You can be debt-free. You can own a great car and a beautiful home. Imagine, all this as possible.

What if instead of thinking "I couldn't" or "I can't," you START THINKING, "I COULD" or "I can?" How might your life be different in a positive way? What if you created space, actually gave yourself some space, to allow for other possibilities? How freeing would it be? IMAGINE THAT!

Belief Creates The Actual Fact

Can you GIVE YOURSELF PERMISSION to believe things differently? What would life be like if you had all the love, health, wealth and success you could find in life? Would you allow it? What if you could be truly happy in spite of any difficulty? Imagine your life differently!

If you could be and believe anything you wanted what might that be? What if you believed the exact opposite of what you already hold to be true? Can you entertain this notion for a little while? What might your life look like, sound like and feel like if you believed things more positively and productively more of the time? Go ahead. Visualize it!

Some people wear their beliefs as tight, clingy clothing. They may be better served to wear a more relaxed, loose fit. If you don't believe you can get good things without suffering look around and find examples of others who have plenty of good things. You can too! There are people who are rich and don't work as hard as those who are poor. How about you? Imagine you could be rich without hard work.

Always Believe Something Wonderful Is About To Happen

Some people find love, quite easily. They have enduring and rewarding relationships. How about you? Can you easily attract the love of your life? What do you think? Do you think you could believe that? Could you do that? Could you easily replace your beliefs that you have held for a long time with other beliefs? Do you think it would be difficult to do or easy? Because whatever you think, you are right.

How you answer, mostly stems from your mindset, your model, your beliefs and attitudes of what is and isn't possible, what is or isn't likely, what you can or can't do easily. If you want your life to change you have to CHANGE SOME THINGS IN YOUR LIFE. Really, you must.

Play with this. Notice what it is like to entertain other possibilities. Do you prefer these? If so, adopt them. If not, let them go. Realize any time you try something new on you might not be immediately comfortable. It may take some time to get used to. Remember, Elvis and the white sequined clothing I mentioned earlier?

To Succeed We Must First Believe We Can

A really good attorney or debater can argue passionately and persuasively for both sides. In order to be congruent and believable the person must adopt the mindset that what he or she believes is the truth. Not only, is it the truth, but it is right to have that belief. They believe in their right to believe it.

You can do this exercise. Try on new, positive, beneficial, supportive beliefs that may counter or challenge some of your chronic, previous, past conditioning. Discover what it is like to believe things differently. Walk a mile in other shoes, instead of your well-worn ones. Try them on and discover.

Don't be too hasty. Sometimes getting comfortable takes a little time. It's okay. Walk a mile in someone's shoes. Why a mile? Because it takes some time to get used to. Some people have difficulty falling asleep in a hotel bed, or in a guest room, because it isn't their bed. It takes time for some people. It's okay.

The Goal Is To Feel Good Most Of The Time

They aren't used to it. It is foreign, unfamiliar and not comfortable. Sometimes, it takes a while to enjoy a new food or beverage. You don't instantly enjoy it. However, the more you taste it the more it grows on you. Sometimes you need to do it more than once. Give the new beliefs a little time to discover if they fit.

Play with them. Live from them. Find out if they serve you better. ENJOY THE EXPLORATION. Have fun, be gentle and explore your limitations and what it is like to GO BEYOND LIMITA- TIONS into whole new areas. Explore! Discover! Adventure. Get really curious. Become fascinated. Do it! Really.

It can be glorious and it can be a little frightening. Whatever it is, is what it is. Whatever it is, it is, all okay. Celebrate it and you will discover many nuances you might not have otherwise noticed. Find the nuances. In fact, celebrate everything! The more you celebrate the more you discover to celebrate!

As You Believe So You Are

Tony's Example: Tony, one of my editors, shared this with me. While he was editing this chapter he decided to take my advice about clothing and beliefs literally. He had always had a problem of getting up early. Tony is self-employed, so if not careful, getting up early can slip away from him. It was particularly difficult if there were no pressing appointments.

Still, Tony wanted to get up early. He said, "It makes for better days." I agree with him about that. He went on to share this with me. He took out a set of pajamas he had, but had not worn in a long time "I imbued them with the belief that I get up at the alarm, or even earlier."

That is what he made himself believe when he wore them. "I emotionalized it, and I saw it vividly," Tony says. "I treat these pajamas with reverence at all times. When not wearing them, I roll them up neatly and place them into a fancy wicker basket, where I made them fit snugly. I positioned this on a nicely made bed and it has worked perfectly."

The More You Do The More You Are Able To Do

"When I wear them I'd get up even before the alarm goes off. How well did it work? He goes on to say, "after a little while I didn't even need to wear them anymore to get the same result. Sometimes, <u>if</u> it wears off I put the special pajamas back on and wake up right on time." Now that is using this material in positive and useful way. If Tony can do something like this and make it work, imagine what you can do!

An important point to notice, is, if there is a time when it doesn't work as he had hoped, he doesn't get upset and throw in the towel. He returns to the practice that worked for him and continues to get the results. This is how you create new and useful habits. You continue to repeat the successful behaviors until they become automatic. When challenges arise, you persist. Keep the commitment and move forward.

Enjoy today. Look for all of the good things!

"Where are you? Here. What time is it? Now. What are you? This moment."
—— Dan Millman

"You were not born with the habit of brushing your teeth. With persistent action, over a period of time, you developed the habit. Now, I'll bet you would never consider going a week without brushing.
—— Paul R. Scheele

"Gratitude is the single most important ingredient to living a successful and fulfilled life."
—— Jack Canfield

CHAPTER SEVEN

Your Mindset Is Crucial

What is your mindset? How is your attitude? Are you a victim or a victor? The difference is in how and what you think. What are your predominant thoughts? Henry Ford said, "Whether you think you can or you think you can't, you are right."

Someone else said, "Your attitude determines your altitude". Do you have a champion's attitude or not? Perspective makes all the difference. When you are open to change anything is possible. Remember, my invitation to you, earlier, was to remain open to concepts, learning and change. How have you been doing?

The following is a story about three clients that Atticus met at the beginning of his law career. Note that his name and the names of the clients and minor details have been changed to protect privacy.

Three people who taught me an important lesson:

Client #1 – Sue

Sue broke her thumb while working. She had a workers compensation claim for this injury. Workers compensation claims are either settled by the parties or determined by the judge. The case value is based upon a chart table that shows values for each part of the body.

Injury severity is rated with percentage numbers, and values are based upon body part and percentage. The maximum thumb value at the time was $10,200.00 if the thumb were amputated. A broken thumb is worth less money. This was literally my smallest case.

Sue wanted me to file a Social Security Disability claim for her. Social Security Disability requires proving to a Judge that she is totally disabled from doing any type of work and therefore unemployable. Sue was also concerned that the doctors to whom her employer sent her for treatment might kill her in order to avoid paying her claim.

As You Believe So You Are

In short, Sue considered her injury to be quite serious and catastrophic.

Client #2 – Juanita

Juanita was also a workers compensation client. At the time of her injury, Juanita was a 16 year old immigrant who worked in a warehouse. She suffered a 20ft fall off of a cherry picker. She broke the fall with her face on cement. She broke every bone in her face. She went blind in one eye and was left with 50 percent vision in her other eye.

You Become What You Think About Most Of The Time

She had to have a steel rod put in her arm. She also incurred brain injury, neck and spine damage, hence she now gets migraines. Her injuries were so substantial that even though I was accustomed to reading serious injury reports, I cringed when I read the medicals.

Prior to the injury, her only education was an 8th grade education that she received in Mexico. She primarily spoke Spanish. I first met Juanita about three years after her injury. She might have had an excellent case for total disability, but Juanita's choices were not helping her case. Unlike Sue, Juanita did not regard her injuries as catastrophic. She learned English and got her high school GED. She found a job using her one good arm to stock shelves in a supermarket.

Although, I considered it puzzling given her limited vision, she told me that she was taking classes for jewelry design. She certainly was not going to make it easy for me to make a claim for total disability based upon her being unable to work. Unlike Sue, Juanita never considered her injuries to be something that would stop her.

People Don't Improve Because They Don't Believe They Can

Client #3 – Tom

Tom was in his 50's. While working in a factory, he was exposed to a dangerous mold called Aspergillus, and the Aspergillus got into his lungs. Getting Aspergillus in your lungs is potentially deadly. A doctor told me that on a pain scale of 1 to 10, Tom was probably at 50. Getting to know Tom was not easy.

It wasn't easy because Tom was always focused on everyone else around him. He had a unique ability to make people feel like royalty. Tom was also not the easiest client. How could I convince anyone that Tom was in great pain while he continued to smile, and seem as happy as someone who just won the lottery.

These three clients taught me that I define the meaning of outside events. I get to choose my attitude and focus. I can magnify a small and temporary problem into a permanent limitation, or I can choose not to let anything stop me.

What You Say Is What You Get

Tom also taught me that even if I'm in great pain, I can spread sunshine wherever I go. No matter how I might feel inside, I can make others feel great. Perhaps, Tom realized that the best way to conceal his pain was to let people believe he was doubled over from laughter, rather than pain.

Thank you Atticus! Here are some thoughts you may wish to incorporate to develop and maintain that winning mindset. These are just samples. Tailor them or create ones that work for you. The key to making affirmations work is to state them emphatically with loads of positive emotion.

While it is true that self-talk has a powerful effect the words aren't nearly as important as the feelings you have while saying affirmations. The emotions are where the actual power comes from. You confirm the affirmations by your attitude. Strong feelings create more strong feelings. You use the words, and create pictures with great feeling.

You Live As Large Or As Small As You Accept – Mindset Matters

HAVE FUN, BE ENTHUSIASTIC and fill your mind and being with positive and powerful thoughts and feelings. Repeat these frequently throughout each day. FEEL MARVELOUS and powerful while speaking, singing or shouting affirmations.

Read these aloud and keep this in mind. If any one of the statements causes you to feel less than glorious, or uncomfortable note that. Notice, if the thought causes discomfort. What does that tell you?

It might suggest you are coming up against one or more previously conditioned beliefs. You might not believe it is okay to feel that way, and that's okay if that occurs for you. You might not believe you embody the feeling or the quality within the affirmation. Again, that is okay. Don't make it an issue

Never Underestimate The Heart Of A Champion – Winners Win

If you state, "I am rich" but you don't feel that, notice it. That is okay. Whatever is going on, is okay but you want to NOTICE AND PAY ATTENTION. You may want to adjust the affirmation so that it feels right. The first step in change is to become aware. You never notice the shoe if it fits. When it doesn't you notice. Get it? So it is good to notice what thoughts make you uncomfortable. It is a signal. That is all.

I will share more on this later but there are a couple things to know that are at work here. One is, you may be coming up against the limitations of your belief system or view of yourself. The belief doesn't match your self-image or concept. One way to BREAK THROUGH is to DO IT anyway. If you do it, repeatedly over and over, with power and conviction, you <u>will</u> come to believe it.

The military knows this. They use cadence, chanting while performing activities and drills. It is an effective mechanism designed to turn young men and women into troops. If it didn't work you can bet they'd abandon it. There is other evidence as well.

Every Champion Was Once A Contender Who Didn't Give Up

A lie repeated often enough, frequently, gets substituted for the truth. People can convince themselves of anything if they say it frequently enough. Just by doing it, as the military has learned, you can come to believe it wholeheartedly. The principle is consistent practice, spaced repeatedly, in time.

Every day, numerous times a day, you can chant, sing, shout and declare. Another bit of evidence comes from eating behaviors and violence studies. People may not like a food at first but after repeated exposure to it can grow to like it. People may abhor crime and violence but after repeated exposure they come to tolerate and in some cases, even accept it as a way of life.

We can learn to accommodate almost anything, good or not so good. Therefore, if you decide to make it a habit, you will accommodate new good habits, too! You will develop these powerful new thought habits using correct practice and spaced repetition. Read through these, then I'll offer some other powerful tips and suggestions. For now, try them on! Try on these new beliefs.

I'm In Charge Of How I Think And Feel I Choose Happiness

"I always move forward to success". "I burn my ship. I leave no way out". "I remain dedicated". "I am passionate". "I am faithful". "I am always convinced, faithful and expectant even when there is no evidence of progress". "Even when it seems the tides are against me and nothing is working, I remain true". Feel invincible and unstoppable as you do these. Either feel it first or get the feeling first.

Either way is fine.

"I intensify my desire for making my dreams come true". "While waiting I make progress every day". "I take action". "I am stead-fast. I know I will prevail". "I make progress during the journey". "I enjoy and celebrate every moment". "My thoughts and my feelings are aligned. I am congruent in my desires". Feel confident and centered, positive and sure. Wrap yourself in the powerful feelings. Feel them fully.

"My concentration, my focus, my energy, is singular and on purpose". "I want being, and doing, and having what I want to be the dominant thoughts in my conscious and unconscious mind". "I want to learn how to be more positive, powerful, and purposeful". "I am accepting, allowing and receptive". "I am magnificent". "I am truly magnificent and invincible". Feel marvelous and filled with joy! Feel! Feel!!

You Are Born To Be A Champion, A Winner

"I go after what I want fully. No way out. No excuses. No doubts or fears, but positive in every atom, every cell, every fiber of my being." "I want to believe in myself and discover that I am truly an emperor inside and out." "I am a winner and a champion." "I am a victor." "I will never allow myself to be a victim of others, circumstances, events, or my own thinking." Imagine it! Feel like a champion, a winner and a victor.

"I will be triumphant." "I will win, conquer and evolve." "I will succeed in ways currently beyond the limits of my imagination and discover myself delighted along the way." "I will celebrate and be grateful for everything always." "Whatever IS, is." "I will look for the good within, and find it." "I will celebrate because that IS what is in the moment."

"What I cannot yet see is all the unexpected good coming my way." "Goodness comes to me." "I always land on my feet." "I always win, even in ways I don't completely understand." "Adversity has always been my friend even when I didn't embrace it." "There is always something marvelous to find. Seek and I will find it. Knock and it will be opened. I do and it is." "I will keep an open mind and an open heart."

To Change Your Life You Need To Change Your Thinking

Read these out loud to yourself daily. Do it morning and before bed if you are able. You might want to record it and play them while wearing headphones. It is your choice. Incorporate these powerful thoughts into you thinking habits.

It is important you BELIEVE AND FEEL GOOD when you state affirmations. If you feel you just can't accept one or another because it is too strongly worded you can work your way up to it. Inch by inch you make your way. You can say, "I am discovering it is okay for me to be a champion". Get it? Change it!

This is actually a way to stay in rapport with yourself. You don't violate any of your beliefs. You put it into the notion of "I am discovering..." or "It is okay for me to discover how incredibly powerful I am". You can say, "I am in the process of discovering that it's wonderful to have lots of money". "I am in the process of discovering it is okay to be powerfully positive". A process is something on going. Use it.

Defeat Is Only Temporary Unless You Quit

We are all in the process of continuing to evolve as people. We are becoming better at getting better. You can affirm this. "I am in the process of feeling magnificent and victorious". Or soften it even more. "I am in the process of learning to feel magnificent and victorious". Get it? If the original affirmation you chose, or any that I have listed, are too strong for you to completely accept and feel good about, use these additional ways to inch your way into it, instead. If the original is too blunt, soften it this way.

You can say "I am learning to be an excellent money manager". "I am learning to become an excellent golfer". "I am in the process of making positive changes in my life". "It's okay that I learn how to assert myself and still be friendly". "I am beginning to feel really confident and powerful". "I am discovering I have many choices". "Feeling powerful is one of the choices I am being to embrace".

"Each day I am learning more and more that I feel good about exercising and coming into my power". "I am enjoying learning how to be magnificent". Get it? You can tailor and create your own paragraphs of affirmations around any important topic area for you. Inch your way into becoming more of that a little bit each day. Eventually, you may SAY, "I AM MAGNIFICENT!!"

Your Decision Keeps You The Same – Or It Moves You Forward

Each morning and evening, and anytime in between, you can take a moment to recite your powerful, positive affirmations, in passionate and enthusiastic ways, do so. This practice can be absolutely LIFE CHANGING in the most amazingly wonderful ways.

You may inch your way or blast your way but if you keep at this, you will get there. Plus, there is a whole lot more you will discover along the way about learning to use these to fashion an absolutely powerful mindset. Attitude is everything. So let your imagination run wild with the many different ways you will put this to good use for yourself.

The rule is this: Within 48 hours of being exposed to new learning material, you must begin to take action steps. Small or large you must do something right away to get the maximum benefit. Get it? I sure hope so. When you do this, you will begin to discover yourself going on the most wonderful drive of your life because you will be in the driver's seat. You want to be the driver. TAKE CHARGE and get going!

Affirm – Declare What Is – Make It Happen – And So It Is

Remember to ask. Seek and continue to knock until you have the response from the universe you seek. Put your order in. Claim it. Wait for it as you do a meal in a cafe. Behind the scenes everything is being prepared. They are making a dish from your orders. They will deliver it. You only need to ENJOY THE TIME WAITING. It is coming! It is yours if you will believe it is yours. Have faith. Claim it.

Editor's note: If you're serious about getting help with your attitude get Rex's "Attitude Activator" on MP3! I copied the link for you to paste if the one above does not work. Enjoy this fabulous program!

https://ideaseminars.mykajabi.com/attitude-activator-special-offer

"You control your future, your destiny. What you think about comes about. By recording your dreams and goals on paper, you set in motion the process of becoming the person you most want to be. Put your future in good hands - your own."
—— *Mark Victor Hansen*

"Productivity is the deliberate, strategic investment of your time, talent, intelligence, energy, resources, and opportunities in a manner calculated to move you measurably closer to meaningful goals."
—— *Dan Kennedy*

"We cannot change what we are not aware of, and once we are aware, we cannot help but change."
—— *Sheryl Sandberg*

"You cannot stop the waves but you can learn to surf."
—— *Jon Kabat Zinn*

Chapter Eight

Make The Law Of Attraction Work

Do you want a happening career? Want to get a great job? Want to book more gigs? Would you like to be happier? Want more money? How about a relationship? Are you interested in the good life?

People try all sorts of things; they work really hard, hope, pray, they bargain, try magic and the Law Of Attraction (LOA). They do lots of different things but seem only to be spinning their wheels.

How do you get what you want? Lots of people work hard but don't get anywhere. They try all those things but still struggle. That is sad. They can have what they want if they learn to work smarter.

Think And Grow Rich

They don't have to work harder. That is a myth. They don't need anything added to them from the outside, but they think they do. So they try lots of things that don't produce the results they want.

I don't really like the term 'the law of attraction' but it has been around for a hundred years or so. Since it is popular and somewhat accurate, I use it to discuss what you can make happen.

The practice is powerful and absolutely works but it is not the 'instant magic pill' people wish it to be. When they find this out 'it' and the reality doesn't match their unrealistic expectations, they quit.

Drop By Drop The Tub Fills – What You Focus On Expands

They blame it for not working, and move on. It's not it that doesn't work. It does. The change that must first take place is an inner change. First, an inner ATTITUDE CHANGE IS NEEDED. Without this, it won't work, that is true.

It isn't magic. It doesn't come from outside of you. No one waves a magic wand. It comes from WITHIN YOU. It is a process and it requires time, so be patient. It is absolutely reliable.

It does work. It is completely up to you. Just don't believe all the hype about 'finding the missing ingredient that wasn't included in 'The Secret'. There is much marketing BS around the LOA.

You Have A Guidance System That Provides Feedback

What is the Law Of Attraction then? It is the harnessing and focusing of your internal mental powers, your feelings and your actions, in pursuit of a strongly desired goal or purpose. Your inner workings determine your outer results.

It includes, the accurate notion that "birds of a feather flock together." "Like attracts like". This isn't magic. This is law! In order to have that happen, you do it. I'll explain.

Simple enough. You PUT YOUR BRAIN TO WORK to deliberately accomplish what it is you want to accomplish. The difference between most people, and those who make it work, is the outer and inner.

Those who have difficulty expect something outside of them to help. They think it comes from elsewhere. Someone, something, or somehow it is made to happen. Those who make the Law Of Attraction work know it is they who help themselves. They get their mindset right AND CREATE what they want.

Change Negativity to Positivity: The Men's Movement

I was called to work with a team of men who were part of a very popular men's movement. They had been having difficulty getting along and moving forward with their agenda for the movement. They asked me to sit in a meeting and then consult with them on how they could be more productive, powerful, and positive.

They had been having great difficulty finding agreement in making things happen and moving the movement and participants forward in a positive direction. I did. I arrived on time, so they knew I was on time and then I excused myself for a while. I left so they would configure the room as they always did. They would sit in the places they normally adopted. I returned later and took a chair near the back.

I watched them say hello, set the meeting, and bicker and bicker. I listened as one idea after the other was brought up and shot down. When their meeting concluded they asked me what I thought.

If What You're Doing Isn't Working – Do Anything Else

I shocked them with what I had to say. I told them they were a bunch of complaining, whining people who were draining the energy out of each other and the team as a whole. I told them they had no means of helping each other or the men's movement by doing what they were doing. To say they shit the floor is another understatement!

They were aghast! I was gentle in my assessment but I did not pull any punches. I told them this was all good news because from that moment on, they could begin to learn to do things in a new way. I informed them that they had an excellent opportunity to transform what they were doing right now into something that would work, both for the committee here today, and for the entire men's movement in the future.

Now they were eager to hear what I shared. I stated it was obvious that they cared for each other and the movement. I pointed out that when they first got together, they did nothing in the way of a ritual or an anchor to make each of them feel positive and optimistic. They entered the room bringing their concerns and baggage. They began by addressing what was wrong, not what was right or what worked well. They were focused on problems and what wasn't working, or what in their opinion wouldn't work.

Stop Reinforcing Negative Habits – Reinforce Positive Habits

They began to realize that by beginning this way they sucked the energy out of each of them and out of the room. They knew this was true. They knew I spoke the truth. I told them exactly like it was. I pointed out that they needed to get together and uplift each other. They should and could build each other up. They could spend time acknowledging and edifying each other.

They could spend time talking about what they liked about each other and what they liked about the movement. They could focus on what they liked about what was going on and begin to look for solutions to the issues from this frame of mind. They would solve problems easier from feeling and being positive and optimistic.

After all, the men's movement was about positively inspiring men to be more at home with oneself and to drop limitations and old conditioning. They could address the 'problems' but not focus on the problems. They needed to redirect their thinking.

Don't Miss The Obvious Because Of The Obvious

By redirecting their thinking, and what they paid attention to, their own energy would change. As a result, their meetings would change and they would infuse positivity and positive energy into the men's movement at large. Then the leadership would be leading from a place of positive power.

I gave them some examples. I taught them anchoring. I gave them some things they could practice. I taught them ways to feel good. I instructed them in how to recall past positive and resourceful experiences that they could focus on and anchor in the present moment. I had them focus on what was good about each of the team members and how blessed they were to work together.

You Make It Happen – You Create It – You Attract It – It Is You

Then they could focus on what they liked, what they wanted, and what they wanted to build in the direction they wanted to move toward. From a state of positivity, they could look at a problem and go 'Here's the issue, now where do I want to go instead?'

I received a lengthy six page letter detailing how they had implemented the suggestions and changes that I had led them through. They were exuberant and grateful that I had helped to reveal their issues, bring clarity to them, and teach them ways to be positive, powerful and effective. They shared with me how it impacted, not only the leadership committee, but also the rest of the men's movement from that day forward, through implementing what I had shared.

Life Isn't What Happens To You – Life Is What You Create

Know this! You can do anything with the right attitude. With the wrong attitude, things can just suck. You have got to come to realize you always have a choice. If you learn nothing ever again, realize this important fact. You can choose. You can choose whether to focus on the good or focus on the not so good. That is your choice always each and every moment of the day.

Remember, you get what you focus on. Energy flows where your attention goes. Thoughts are things. You become what you think about most often. So choose. Choose wisely! If you know nothing else, know this. You can choose where you put your attention and that will make an incredible difference in your life. Start with baby steps if you must, but do it. Get it? Do it!

What You Think About You Bring About

The LOA means you focus on your goal with such DESIRE, such PASSION, that all else falls away. You target your goal with laser like precision. All of YOUR ENERGY is devoted to making this come true.

Your goal begins as an idea you proceed to make real. You create it and fashion it. It is all you. You focus your energies and resources the same way you aim a magnifying glass to focus light and burn paper.

That same paper can sit in unfocused daylight forever and never burn. You focus, you create and you attract because of your mindset and your behaviors, not because of magical wishing things different.

Energy Flows Where Your Attention Goes

YOUR INTENTION and attention is so devoted to what you want, your subconscious works on this day and night and comes up with ideas and plans for how you can accomplish it. You got it serving you.

Marshal your resources and abilities. You don't have to know how to begin because as you act and move forward you initiate these processes. Begin where you are with what you have! You are supported.

'How' will take care of itself as you act on your own behalf. Your subconscious figures things out for you. Get it? Enlist the aid of that part of you that knows far more than you consciously can.

You Don't Live A Positive Life Thinking Negative Thoughts

You may change your plans many times en route to your destination but keep traveling to where you want to go. Don't give up. Don't quit. If obstacles arise and you detour, you detour but keep going. You persist. This is where others throw in the towel. They think it should be easy. They want it easy. They want luck.

It is easy. Not always, but it is. It is simple. When it does get tough, you must too. You are the person in charge. Not a deity or deities, not wishes or magical fairy dust. Your subconscious mind is in charge.

As you journey you begin to understand it is you who are creating success. You also understand success never happens in isolation! If you are smart you will do things that attract and enlist the aid of others. Develop your personality so as to be likable. Develop a pleasing personality so others want to help.

People Don't Improve Because They Don't Believe They Can.

Be sure to apply the Golden Rule. Treat others well! Treat them exceptionally well, first! Treat others with respect. Give them your full, undivided, attention. You help because you like people. No other reason. People will reciprocate. So give and you'll receive. Others will reciprocate, but you go first.

Go the extra mile and add value. Again, you add it FIRST. Help without having to be asked. If you want others to help you it only makes sense you give them something worthy in advance. Get it? Surround yourself with others who are smarter and who can help you on the way.

Support others who are trying to succeed. Celebrate their successes as they move forward. Then they reciprocate! Work together as a team. Become a valued player. Through co-operation we get further, faster than alone or in trying to compete. When we CELEBRATE AND VALIDATE others they do reciprocate! Remember a rising tide floats the whole boat. Help others succeed and they'll help you!

People Don't Improve Because They Don't Believe They Can

With your mind and energies so focused, your brain becomes alerted to others, events and opportunities that are beneficial to you, and you to them. More wonderful things seem to come your way.

Your Reticular Activating System (RAS) in your brain works this way. Because you focused it, it finds matches in your experience and within your memories and out in the 'real' world. You begin to NOTICE OPPORTUNITY previously closed off from you. It really does work this way. Activate it for yourself.

People are attracted to you because you are a more attractive personality. Your friendliness, your commitment, your drive and your passion are attractive to like-minded people. Like attracts like. Like a beacon light on a hill others are drawn to you.

Never forget however, it is you doing it. You are purposefully trans-forming yourself. You are making everything happen. You are working it in smart ways. You are responsible when you TAKE CHARGE!

You Become What You Think About All Day Long

You are a deliberate creator. You, and others, help you succeed. So don't get egotistical about it. Stay humble. Keep focused on all the factors that contribute to your success. Be grateful. Celebrate all.

You started it. You have to maintain it. It is always up to you. Most people expect it to happen to or for them if they believe, pray, chant, affirm, and visualize. It doesn't. That isn't how it works. That isn't the actual Law Of Attraction. You make it happen. You keep it going! What you put out, you get back.

Keep going until you have what you want. You will attract like-minded dedicated people to assist you. Be friendly and cooperative. Value these people you attract. Value your time and energy. Use these wisely to accomplish your dreams.

Birds Of A Feather Flock Together

You'll FIND MORE OPPORTUNITY. You will discover more of the good life. You will notice yourself having more fun, being more delighted and living large. Celebrate it all. Never forget YOU ARE DOING IT. You are doing it! Others are helping and you are helping others.

Take advantage of and, continue to, ENJOY the new GOOD LIFE that seems to comes to you. This is why it does seem magical. You create it but, enjoy the process so much, it seems like magic. You put out the energy first and it is returned.

Consider obstacles as lessons. Learn from those moments. Obstacles are really disguised blessings! All defeat is temporary unless you give up. Stay in the game. Maintain your focus! Keep your positive mental attitude. Persevere and learn! Learn from each and every challenge that comes your way. You don't need to seek challenges out. They will certainly find you. Welcome them when they show up. That is the way!

First Learn To Stand Then Learn Fly – Wax On Wax Off

Maintain your positive productive actions, behaviors and practices. As you do you will develop positive, new and reliable habits. You will begin to eliminate the old worn out ones. It's a conditioning process. You DEVELOP GOOD HABITS. You replace the old, non-supportive conditioned habits with new supportive ones.

Soon, you will delightfully discover, you will have replaced tired, chronic, defeatist thinking with positive powerful, thoughts. You will have transformed your thinking, your feeling, yourself and your life. You will think powerfully. You will feel marvelous. You will take right inspired action, guided by your own subconscious or non-conscious self. You made it happen. So realize this, you make it happen. You will!

You took charge. You lived a champion lifestyle. CELEBRATE! Absolutely celebrate progress along the way. Find moments throughout the day to stop and feel blessed. Appreciate yourself. Enjoy being you! You are doing it. You may not see forward into the future how it will all work out. That is okay!

Look For Smiles At The Start Of Your Day

When you look back later, you can connect the dots and see how you made it happen. That is how it works for all of us. We can connect the dots looking back at the path and see how we got from place to place. While going through it keep your desire and faith high. Keep going no matter what. Are you beginning to understand?

When finished you'll know the Law Of Attraction works. You will have created and attracted what you want. Once you have put it into practice, it is easy to do again and again. The more we do the more we are able to do. Perfect practice makes perfect. You get better by doing. You learn to translate your idea into reality. You learn to get your goals and dreams.

You start small but eventually get to big things. It is the same as developing any skill or talent. As you repeatedly, do it, correctly, you get better at it through time. Repetition is the mother of skill! What is the single best thing you can do to make it all happen?

Live Learn Love Laugh And Celebrate Always

Enjoy the process. Feel blessed. Love yourself. Love each moment and be thankful. Delight and celebrate each step along the way. Celebrate, embrace and learn from every stumble, misstep and fall on the journey. All of it is part of the journey, It is what is! Love it. Accept it! Be thankful. Have fun!

Attitude is everything! Your thoughts become things. Henry Ford said, "If you think you can or you think you can't you are right." I say, "If you believe it will be easy, it will be. If you believe it will be hard, it will be. It will be whatever you believe it to be." It will be whatever you decided it is! Get it? Get it??

Hindsight Is 20/20

Live the life of a creator. LIVE IN GRATITUDE. Feel appreciation. Help others. Most don't and won't ever live this way. They drop out anywhere along the line. They didn't have to. It is just what they did.

Instead of owning up, they blamed the LOA. They say it didn't work. That thinking will never get them what they want because they are not in charge. Some "it" is in charge, but "it" doesn't do the work.

You do! Since you are not like those people, have fun and enjoy. Delight and MAKE MORE MOMENTS MARVELOUS. Have fun and enjoy all the good things you were born to enjoy. The world is your garden. Love it and care for it. CELEBRATE EVERYTHING.

Discover what makes you most totally alive and enjoy it today!

> *"A person's success in life can usually be measured by the number of uncomfortable conversations he or she is willing to have."*
> — *Tim Ferris*

CHAPTER NINE

You Can Make It Better

It always fascinates me how things work out together. Some call it synchronicity. This next topic is on kindness and committing those random acts. When I was planning to write about it, it came home to me in a delightful way.

I was at home. I had dozed off. I was awakened gently by my daughter who said, 'I brought you soup.' Wonderful, I thought. Plus, she brought home something for me to drink. I'm delighted. It is welcomed and it was tasty.

I felt well taken care of and loved. We talked as I ate soup. It came out that out she has been delivering soup to a friend's grandmother for a number of weeks. She had visited once and discovered the woman's refrigerator bare.

If You Want To Lift Yourself Up Lift Up Someone Else

She had a couple eggs, cheese, and nothing in the freezer. My daughter took some soup over the next evening and the woman enjoyed it. So my daughter made it more of a regular thing. She'd take her a quart or two of soup. She liked being able to help out and know that the woman was eating.

Nightly, after work, she'd tell me she was going to this woman's house. Even in very bad weather she made the delivery. I had been concerned at times when weather was rough. I wanted her to come home safe, but she would say she was going to her friend's grand-ma's house first.

I never knew why until tonight. It simply came up as we chatted and I ate the soup she brought me. After some more conversation she stated she was excited about our plans for the next evening. Off to her room she went. I am blessed with two wonderful children. I was well taken care of this late night.

Focus On What You Can Change

I am very proud. My daughter simply wanted to do something nice for this woman because she cared. She told me the woman has a job and works hard but has a difficult time making ends meet. She can't make enough money to buy much food. My daughter cared! She acted!

When people care for other people, we lift each other up. We ought to assist people without criticizing them for their lot in life. We help them because of what is in our heart, not because of what they can do in return. We go the extra mile for others because we are able to. We should let compassion rules us.

I think this is what life is really all about. Simple kindness. Goodness toward each other. We are all on this rock encased by clouds, together. We ought to be able to get along, help and enjoy each other.

You Don't Need A Reason To Help People

Let your actions be your reward, not the praise from others. It feels good to DO SOMETHING NICE. It is increase for all! A rising tide floats the boat and everyone in it. Instead of dying, it promotes thriving. Simple acts of kindness can go a long way toward helping us, help people.

We should help others feel exalted, honored, revered and respected. We should strive to lift each other up together instead of tearing each other apart or down. More kindness is needed, less greed and intolerance. Do what you can to help another and you help yourself. Be nice. Be friendly. Be open and available. Be generous.

When you give you get back. It may not come back in the form you'd expect but it does come back. I practice tipping better, whether they deserve it or not. I am not interested in sending a message about poor service. I simply want to delight another person when I am able to. I tip better, coming from a place of abundance, and I want to spread that around.

The other day I ordered take out. When I arrived, the food was ready sooner than I expected. Paying the bill took quite a long time. I returned home to discover they didn't include enough rice for all the meals. I called and they said come back and they would provide much more. This meant another 30 minute round trip while guests waited. I made the trip.

You Can Think And Grow Rich

Once I returned to the restaurant, getting the rice took forever. I had the same service person as earlier. I knew this was a trying day for her. So, when I got the additional rice I gave her a hefty tip just to put a smile on her face. I share this, not to put myself in a positive light, but to simply show how life offers us numerous opportunities.

I could have been all upset about the take-out delays. I could let that "spoil my day". Some would. Sometimes, one event is enough to set someone off for a long while. One event shouldn't contaminate everything else, but some of us let it. So I had a choice. We all do. Be upset or help another person feel a little bit better. I chose the latter. This made me feel good, too.

Do what you can. I did what I could. I couldn't make her entire day all better, but I could be pleasant and put a smile on her face. Do whatever is right for you. Be led by your heart. As you do, you will discover so much goodness surrounding you, it might floor you. It is there. It is always there! Sadly, some miss it.

Joseph Murphy wrote the following: "There is no one to change but yourself. You have to BE NICE TO YOURSELF; the real self of you is God. Exalt, honor, revere and respect this Divine Presence within yourself; then you love and honor your neighbor. Your neighbor is the closest thing to you; God is your neighbor; and if you love God you will have goodwill toward all men."

When Life Knocks You Down - Get Up Or Give Up

It is good to uplift others. When you put it out there you get it back in countless untold ways. Simply make it a point to be friendly, gentle, accepting, kind, peaceful and loving. The more love and goodness we spread around the more we get back to enjoy and spread again.

Create that ambience around you. And know this: People are mostly good! We hear about the bad ones all the time in media, but mostly, people are wonderful! We all should keep that in mind. What we focus on we get back. Let's FOCUS ON GOODNESS. Let's build what we want to have more of. Let's celebrate everything!

Today is another day to be thrilled!

"People often say motivation doesn't last. Well, neither does bathing. That is why we recommend it daily."
— *Zig Ziglar*

"The ability to discipline yourself to delay gratification in the short term in order to enjoy greater rewards in the long term, is the indispensable prerequisite for success."
— *Brian Tracy*

CHAPTER TEN

Do Your Beliefs Serve You?

Growing up, my main idol was Harry Houdini, escape artist extraordinaire. He was a magician and an escape artist who died in 1926, but whose name is used nearly daily to describe incredible feats. His name is both a noun and a verb in the dictionary. To 'do a Houdini' or 'get Houdinied' describes incredible performance feats. It means to extricate oneself from a difficult situation. It is used almost daily in media.

What does he have to do with our thoughts? Great thought leaders from ancient times through today have pointed out that our only limitations exist in our thinking and what we believe. If we think we can or we can't, we are right. I repeat. The only limitations we have, or encounter, exist solely in our thinking.

Thinking makes it so. Whatever we focus on expands. If we are predominantly negative or don't think we can, we won't. If we don't believe we can make things happen or design a life to live on our own terms, then it is unlikely we will ever do so. Thoughts stop us, if we let them. Stop letting thoughts stop you!

A Breakthrough Occurs - The Impossible Becomes Possible

Houdini made a name for himself by going around the USA and other countries offering to escape from their jail cells. He challenged the police to restrain him, and constrain him, in such a way that he could not get free. He offered cash rewards to those who could hold him.

He never had to pay. He escaped. He knew what he was doing and beyond that he was a master marketer and publicist. He knew how to get attention. He escaped from countless jail cells worldwide.

In one jail, he was stripped naked, as usual. Searched, to make sure he had no keys or lock picks and then shackled. The cell door was closed and locked. The jailers and press left the area. Houdini was alone in the cell. If everything went according to plan Houdini would get free from the shackles and the cell.

The Kite Rises Highest Against The Wind

Minutes later Houdini would emerge dressed and holding the shackles. The press and jailers would go wild. He escaped the locked cell. He always had! He had never been defeated. Except, this time something was going horribly wrong. Houdini, now inside a cell, his jailers gone, works on the cell lock.

He can't pick it! He used hidden picks, but today it was not working. An hour went by and he began to panic. He had never encountered a jail cell lock he couldn't pick. He kept trying. His entire reputation was on the line. If he failed his career was over. He couldn't pick it. He fought against the panic.

Another hour passed. He was covered in sweat. Afraid. Near exhaustion, he collapsed against the jail cell door. It swung open. What? It swung open! The jailers, in all the commotion, had forgotten to lock the door. They simply shut it and left the room. No one realized.

The Mind That Perceives The Limitation Is The Limitation

Not even Houdini. He couldn't pick the lock open because the lock was already open. Shocked, but relieved, he quickly dressed and exited the cell triumphant. Headlines in the paper praised his escape.

Only Houdini knew the truth until he revealed it years later. He was a prisoner of his own mind. He thought the door was locked.

That is the same with each of us. We are prisoners of our own limiting thoughts and beliefs. We have assumptions we grew up with that go unchallenged. We think we can't or are not good enough. We must stop believing the limitations and instead challenge them.

However, we can't or won't challenge them if we aren't aware that we have them, or what they are. That is why earlier I asked you to explore the beliefs you hold and to try on different sets of assumption. You were to write them down so you could work with them. If you didn't, go back and do it now.

Life Becomes Limitless When You Become Fearless

Have you ever got in your car and discover a fly or bee had been trapped in there during the hours you were gone? You roll down all your windows but the insect doesn't leave. You try driving at high speed hoping that it might some how get sucked out. Sometimes, that actually works.

The reason the bee or fly doesn't leave is because it flies around, banging into the windows, bumping up against the glass and at some point determines the boundaries are its limits. You may have noticed the same thing when a fly gets trapped between your screen and home window. Even though you open the window the fly doesn't leave that area. In fact, I have discovered dead flies in the sill with the window or screen open. They make a premature commitment about the boundaries of their known universe.

They do this in their tiny brains. Once the limits become set they don't traverse them. They 'believe' they can't so they don't try any more or attempt to go further. It is called, a premature cognitive commitment. It is premature because it is early. It is cognitive because it uses the brain. It is a commitment because we get locked into it.

If What You're Doing Isn't Working - Do Anything Else

You train fleas the same way. If you ever saw a flea circus all those fleas remain inside their containers without lids. Want to train some? Get an aquarium and some fleas, or flies. Put a glass plate on top large enough to cover the entire opening. Wait a couple hours or days and remove the glass cover. 95-99% of all the fleas or flies will remain inside the aquarium. They won't go past where the cover was.

The circus trains elephants in the same manner. When the elephant is young they use a heavy chain staked to the ground. The young elephant pulls against the chain to no avail. It learns the limits. Later the chain is replaced with a flimsy rope. The adult elephant remains because of its premature cognitive commitment. Horses work the same way. Riders just loop the reigns over a bar and the horse remains tethered.

It is considered a premature commitment because none of the animals know that later the circumstances will change. They accept the limitations and are governed by these mental commitments after the circumstances are altered; the windows opened, the glass removed, the rope replaces the chain. Fortunately, for Houdini, he fell against the door about the time he was giving up.

If You Always Do What You Always Did – You Get What You Got

We are governed by past conditioning in a similar manner. Unless, we become aware of the limitations in our thinking we will continue to be ruled by it.

Once we become aware and we change the circumstances, we can then change the conditioning. We re-condition our minds to be supportive and GO BEYOND THE PREVIOUS LIMITS. The key is learning to let go and drop less than supportive thought habits.

It's time for a review. Our brains are amazing. They are designed or evolved to work in incredible ways. Remember the Reticular Activating System (RAS). It is so important that I want to continue to discuss it.

You Get What You Think About

The RAS is a part of your brain, located in the back of your skull near the brainstem. Its job is to help you stay safe and survive and to remain consistent. It helps you to continue to do what you have always done.

It says, "yes" to you. Whatever you say, it says "yes" to, and finds matches, or supporting evidence, inside you, and past experience. For example; if you say, "gosh, I am so stupid" or "I am so clumsy", your brain will go on a search for you. Your brain will look for all the memories, associations, experiences where you acted 'dumb' or clumsily.

It will offer these up to your conscious mind for you to recall and feel even more dumb or clumsy. That is how it works. If you said, "I am so smart" it would do the same. It also searches for matches in the outer world. An example of this is when you buy new clothes or a car or something important to you.

What You Focus On Expands – You Get What You Focus On

Then you notice your recent purchase all over the place, in the real world. You hadn't noticed them before. They were always there you just didn't PAY ATTENTION. Until, it became important to you, you didn't notice. Once important, then suddenly you notice your purchase everywhere.

The working of the RAS allows the mind to newly recognize things that were practically invisible before. After a new understanding or decision, as if by magic, things relating to them are detected all around. They were always there but went unnoticed.

This has very much to do with beliefs. Why not examine some of yours, again? We have beliefs about everything. Take a look inside to DISCOVER whatever it is you find. You will find plenty, I am sure.

If You Think You Can Or You Think You Can't You're Right

We have beliefs about who we are; what we are capable of and what we are not capable of. We have beliefs about family, friends, relationships, finances, health, career, job, the economy, the future, the past, other people, the government, the world, the weather, god, education, medicine, leisure and so many more areas. Whew! You name it we believe something about it.

Our BELIEFS tend to be POSITIVE or Negative. They tend to be statements such as "I can" or "I can't". They can be in the form of rules and regulations as when you think, "there ought to be a law" or "people should just know better". They can be phrased as "I will" or "I won't".

The words "ought to" or "should", ought to or should tip you off a belief statement follows. These are rules or beliefs about yourself and what you 'should do or could do'. There are rules, beliefs, 'shoulds', and judgments you hold others to. These may not be the same ones you apply to yourself. You may hold others to a different standard than you hold yourself to. It's means, "do what I say, but not as I do."

A belief statement may follow after the word "because". "Because" is a reason you provide. All of our reasons tend to be what we believe is the case. From, why we are late to why we are broke, we have plenty of reasons. We have beliefs about cause and effect. Beliefs tend to be assertions or declarations. Usually, any statement that begins with "I am" or "I have", clue you in, that a belief follows those words.

Some things we believe strongly and passionately. We fight about these at times. Others we hold less closely. Regardless, beliefs make up our map of the world and how we navigate it. Believe it or not, humans do navigate the world by a map. We use inner maps just as we us maps in the outer world. Beliefs are an important part of that map.

Believing Is Seeing

Beliefs determine what we allow in and consider and what we don't and won't. They determine how big or small our abilities are as well as how large our world is. Our beliefs affect us in so many ways and at so many levels it is useful to uncover what it is we believe.

Some are very obvious, up front and in your face beliefs while others cluster around hanging out barely in sight. Both kinds affect us! Go ahead and examine, reflect, look at, introspect on what you believe about yourself.

Exercise: Write down the beliefs you discover. Write as many as you can. Put them into pro and con lists, as supportive or not supportive. Some will be enabling while others disabling. Ask yourself, "Does this belief serve me? If so, how?" Write it down. If it doesn't write it down. Decide as you go along, with each belief. Is this belief one you want to keep? Decide which ones you would prefer to let go? Let those go!

Speak What You Seek Until You See What You've Said – Create

There may be clusters of beliefs around certain areas that seem to support each other or come out in a flood. Others, you may have to tease out one by one. When I say cluster or belief cluster I mean similar to a bunch of grapes. There are many different single grapes that make up the bunch.

Belief clusters are similar in that single beliefs support other single beliefs. So, around any topic area you may or will have multiple intersecting and supporting beliefs. You may even have ones diametrically opposed, which can cause internal conflict or dissonance.

What do you believe? Some people will sit and fret thinking it is difficult to find beliefs. That would be your first belief to start with then! Others will find this quite easy. Some beliefs are situational, or contextual, while others, you may think, are important and apply for all time and space; and for everyone.

What You Believe Is What You Get

You may have heard the story of a mother and daughter cooking ham. Mom cuts off the tips of the ham and places it in a pan then into the oven. The young girl asks, "Why did cut you off the ends of the ham?" "That is what my mother always did." "Yes, but why?" the youth persisted.

"I don't know exactly, let's call Grandma." They do and Grandma says, "I don't know. That is how my mother always did it when she cooked one." "Let's call Great Grandma," squeals the little girl. On the phone, Great Grandma says, "Ohhhh, I cut the ends off because my pan was too small for a whole ham to fit."

Some things we do, some things we believe. We don't even know why we do. A clue that a belief is being expressed is when someone uses the words, if, then, always, never, each, every, everybody, has to, should, must, or that makes, or that means. Whatever follows these words is a belief statement or reveals a belief lurking nearby. A belief can be considered a generalization or a rule, or rules we adhere to.

You Become What You Think About Most Often Each Day

For example: "All children under the age of 12 must be taught manners so they behave appropriately in life. Everybody knows this is true. Kids, always tend to get into trouble unless controlled from early on. If you take charge and teach them correctly they will learn better. That means they have a better chance at being successful in life. Those who never get ahead are usually hooligans. If you don't do this it means you don't care and the children will suffer. It is important to do things right. You should care about what you do."

Get it? None of these statements are necessarily true or false. They could be either. However, someone could believe this. Others, might not. Beliefs and reasons do not have to be true at all for us to hold onto them strongly. We believe the most ridiculous things sometimes. The reasons we think we do things aren't even necessarily accurate.

Check into it. It is an important area that affects each one of us. So do some exploring, learn a little bit more about you, and enjoy the process!

Split-brain researcher and pioneer Michael Gazzaniga, came to the conclusion there is a "reason center" of the brain. After years of working with patients, who had the thick bundle of nerves connecting both of their brain hemisphere severed, Gazzaniga concluded the brain had a job to just come up with reasons for things. The reasons it produces, that we adhere to, are not necessarily accurate. It is just a part of brain function. He has many publications and books. You may find some of his work and research fascinating.

What You Focus On Expands

Examine your beliefs and reasons. Chuck the ones that don't support you and don't serve you in being your best self and creating your best life. Make a commitment to you! Challenge yourself to grow and transform. You can and will. Just don't let bad reasons and limiting beliefs prevent you. Instead, learn to choose what you want to believe.

Put those beliefs and reasons to work that serve and support you! Get it? Make each moment marvelous.

"Don't wait until everything is just right. It will never be perfect. There will always be challenges, obstacles and less than perfect conditions. So what? Get started now. With each step you take, you will grow stronger and stronger, more and more skilled, more and more self-confident and more and more successful."
— *Mark Victor Hansen*

"If you would take, you must first give, this is the beginning of intelligence."
— *Lao Tzu*

CHAPTER ELEVEN

Beliefs And Feelings Matter

What we believe is critical to our success and our happiness in all facets of life. Beliefs are really nothing more than thoughts or clusters of thoughts we think over and over that result in feelings. We can divide beliefs into two main categories: Supportive or non-supportive beliefs.

Beliefs tend to keep us the same or consistent. They can be limiting or non-supportive which keep us stuck, with no movement, or supportive ones, which help us, move forward.

According to estimates, we habitually think more than 60,000 thoughts a day. That's quite a few thoughts. Many are frivolous or distractions but some of these 60,000 thoughts produce powerful feelings!

Believing Is Seeing - Perception Is Everything

We can't possibly keep track of all our thoughts. The good news is we can use our feelings to figure out what we are thinking. If we FEEL GOOD we are thinking positive and along the lines of what we want or what we want to include. We are moving forward.

If we feel less than glorious it is a good bet we are focused on what we don't want or what we want to exclude from our lives and we may feel stuck.

The goal is to FEEL GOOD MOST OF THE TIME. Why, because one it feels good! Duh. Two when you feel your best you are mentally, emotionally, spiritually, physically, more able to CREATE AND ATTRACT what you want. When you are on top of the world everything tends to work together. You are in flow.

Winners Fail But Don't Quit — They Fall But Get Up

So when we discover we are not feeling good then it is up to us to change our thoughts, or beliefs, to more positive ones. The negative feelings we have are a signal to change our thought patterns. Isn't it nice to have a built-in signal that alerts us it is time to change? Feelings are our signal system, so pay attention to how you feel.

It will let you know whether you are thinking positive thoughts and beliefs, or not. So, when you are feeling less than glorious, check and change your thinking. Use the signal to make the positive changes to get back on track and feeling good. Inch by inch if necessary.

When negative events occur what should you think, and do, about them? Do you spend time wondering why they happen? That would be a waste of your time. Instead use them to transform yourself.

I Never Met A Strong Person With An Easy Past

How can you TRANSFORM YOURSELF so you can enjoy better things, events and circumstances? This will help clarify some important concepts.

Bad things are blessings! Just as negative feelings are blessings that help you turn your attention to the positive, bad events can help you refocus your thoughts and beliefs, your feelings and actions so you get better results.

This may seem difficult to comprehend but you will benefit greatly, once you are able to embrace this.

'Bad things' help you to know what you do want. Whenever 'bad things' or negative thoughts occur you think or say, "I don't want this." Actually you probably swear a lot but it is the same thing. You don't want it.

Winners Fall But Get Up

What do you want instead? This moment, is an opportunity to find, and focus on, what you want, and make what you want, begin to happen. Immediately ask, "WHAT DO I WANT?" Focus on this. Then, instead of wasting your time with unproductive thinking, or hoping things change, start committing. Decide to be different!

Hope is fine, but wishing and hoping won't change things. Resolve to make it different. Decide. Commit. Find, what you want. CLARIFY IT. Specify what you want. Focus on that. Decide to bring it about. Think, 'I am going to do this, that's it! I'm going to make this happen!'

Stop being a victim of negativity and circumstances. Resolve that YOU ARE BIGGER THAN ANY OBSTACLE. Mindset is important! Fix your mind on the positive good you want! Determine to make it happen. Become invincible. Marshal all of your positive resources. It's up to you!

You're The Product Of Your Decisions

Don't worry about how you will do it. First, DECIDE TO DO IT. The how will come after you make the decision and begin taking action. You go as far as you can see, and when you get there, you will see farther. Get it? You are the force that changes things for the better.

If it is going to change for you, you are going to make the changes. You are the one who makes the difference. Get this right! YOU ARE THE POSITIVE, POWERFUL, FORCE IN YOUR LIFE, or you are not. Which is it? Make the decision to take charge. Set your attitude. It's everything! Believe in yourself. That's what all this work on beliefs is for.

When you focus solidly on what you want, when you know precisely what you want, your subconscious, looks for opportunities, you would otherwise miss, while preoccupied with negative events and thoughts. When you change your mindset, EVERYTHING CHANGES!

Joy Is A Decision – Happiness Is A Choice – Decide To Live Well

Move forward. Be willing to make good happen. Begin now. Focus on the good. Be grateful for the opportunity. Consider the negative events, not as negative, but as a blessing for you to get clear and make good things happen. Feel the gratitude. Feel the resolve. Feel the energy and flow. When you do EVERYTHING CHANGES! Energy flows where your attention goes. Celebrate everything!

Exercise: Whenever you become aware of being less than glorious in your thoughts or speech, whenever you think or feel or act, or life delivers you events and circumstances you do not want, STOP, and take a breath. Create a momentary pause and then ask yourself, "What do I want right now?" or "What do I want?" Then DECIDE what it is you do want, instead of what was offered. Focus on what you do want.

AFFIRM what you want. Let go of what you don't want. ACT in a POSITIVE, productive way. Make what you want happen. Act immediately. Anytime life offers you what you don't want, ask "What do I want?" and then work to bring that about.

Make today a spectacular day!

Look at your life as an experiment. Make a (compromise) with all your doubts and fears: For a year or two, do what you can to move toward your ideal scene, in an easy and relaxed manner, in a healthy and positive way. See what happens."
— *Mark Allen*

"In life you need either inspiration or desperation."
— *Tony Robbins*

"What we learn with pleasure we never forget."
— *Alfred Mercier*

CHAPTER TWELVE

The Incredible Power Of Movement

You have been learning that YOU CAN CHANGE how you feel by changing your thoughts and beliefs. Mindset and attitude determine how you feel. Whatever thought you think causes you to feel a particular way. If negative you will feel negative.

How you feel then determines your next thought, which will then be more negative. You spiral down. If the thoughts and feelings were positive you would spiral up into feeling better.

Your thoughts lead to feelings, which determine what actions you take. The actions you take determine the results you get. When you notice you are feeling bad change YOUR THOUGHTS to get different feelings, actions and results.

Don't Miss The Obvious – Become Aware

You can also CHANGE YOUR FEELINGS to change your thoughts. Begin with your body to make the change in your thinking. People have been told, since ancient times that working in a garden, or hard physical work, will resolve depression. It is true.

When you move your body vigorously, or in certain ways, you release different chemicals in the brain. You use different neural pathways. Therefore, you can change how you use your body TO FEEL DIFFERENTLY and THINK DIFFERENTLY.

You have heard of a runner's high? Running and certain activities become addictive because of the release of endorphins, which make us feel good. When you feel good you think clearer and better. That is why running, jogging and even walking can clear a mood. So consider using your body to feel and think better.

Stop Reinforcing Negative Habits – Reinforce Positive Habits

Because we become what we think about, we will become less than glorious if most of our thoughts are less than glorious. The reverse is true, too. If we think better thoughts we will feel better. It works both ways. So, do whatever it takes to build the habit of self-correcting. Discover that you can FEEL GREAT most of the time.

There is a saying, "Standing Is Harder Than Walking." It is true. Have you ever noticed? Try standing still for any amount of time. There is a tendency to move, to fidget, or to squirm.

We want to move. If we can't move large muscle groups we might blink more, or twitch small muscle groups. We want to move. We were designed to move.

Standing IS Harder Than Walking

It is easier to make progress and to change than it is to remain stuck or still. Our natural inclination is for progress and movement. We grow and develop. We learn. It feels better. That is why being stuck is yucky.

Being stuck takes its toll just as standing takes its toll on the muscles. Being sedentary exacts a toll on the body and our health. We evolved to move most of the daylight hours.

The physical way to end being stuck is to create more movement in your body. Do more of following things. When you do you create more movement in your mind, so you STOP GETTING STUCK.

Become Alert – Become Aware – There Are Infinite Possibilities

Move, walk, skip, dance, breathe differently, get a massage or play with a child or a pet. Do anything to help you feel a bit better. The point is to make changing from less than glorious to glorious a habit. Bit by bit, step by step. Tiny doesn't matter. It is good. Little adjustments, over time, are incredibly powerful.

SHIFT YOUR BODY and use your physiology TO FEEL BETTER. Isn't this great news? It is very important to know and utilize. When feeling down or negative do something physical. Stretch become more flexible. Do yoga. Walk, Rebound. Do a few minutes of morning exercise to get going!

Move your body throughout the day. Move your body to change from a less than glorious mood to a more glorious mood. Go for a swim, walk in the pool, skip, and dance, do aerobics. Get moving. Get your body moving and you mind will start moving. Put your focus on the physical and the mental will let go. Exercise is good for the body and the brain. KEEP MOVING it!

Today Do One Thing To Take Care Of You Do It Again Tomorrow

Walking is excellent for overall well-being. You will increase your stamina and become more fit but not more muscular. Walking an hour a day or more is desirable. Stand when you can. If you sit a lot during your day, attempt to get up every 20 minutes or so. Don't sit for long periods.

Change your physiology. Throw your shoulders back, put your chest out, your chin forward and sit, stand, move and walk as if you felt confident, positive and powerful. You can get down and roll around and PLAY as a little child would. You can move your body differently

Breathe. Breathe. Take deep breaths. Get fresh air. Take a pause to breathe.

When You're Stuck In Your Own Loop Change It

If you work on computer a lot, take an eye break, about every 20 minutes. Look as far off as you can. Look all the way out the window or across the room. Shift your focus to the distance. Rest your eyes. Relax. When walking outdoors gaze off into the distance. Look at the horizon if you can. Allow yourself to OPEN UP AND BE MORE EXPANSIVE.

Smile more. Laugh more. Have fun taking care of yourself. Approach it lovingly. Gift yourself when you do things in your best interest. Not all the time, but every so often, reward yourself for accomplishing something you set out to do. Enjoy the reward. Pat yourself on the back. Think, "Good job!"

LOVE AND APPRECIATE YOUR BODY AND YOUR MIND. Appreciate yourself for taking care of you. Assist your body in taking care of you by maintaining a positive mindset and a lit inner light or spirit. Have fun. Play games. Skip, sing, dance, play music. Do yoga. This is the key!

What You Say Is What You Get – Control Your Self Talk

Bit by bit do things that bring the body and mind more energy. I repeat, go for a walk barefoot. Connect with the earth. Lie on a beach or in a nice natural setting. Work in the garden. Gardening is sage advice, because we connect with the earth and we get our hands dirty. When we are preoccupied with troubles or feeling down go into the garden. Concentrate on life in the garden. It works wonders!

Remember, stuck implies no movement. It means, remaining the same as if frozen. In order to break free we need to move and change things up. We can do almost anything and bring about some positive results. If you always do what you always did you always get what you always got. Get it?

If you can't leap into things, at least, inch your way into them. Both ways are effective and can bring dynamic results. The point is, you must do something. Start early, before it is too late, is a wise approach. Prepare before it is required, and you will be well served.

You Can't Live A Positive Life With A Negative Mind

Shake it up. Vary it. This is why you STRETCH A LITTLE and do some light yoga, breathing, or any form of exercise. If you are low energy, do that which brings energy to you. Move and gradually increase the variety and the intensity of your movement. Walk. Skip. Run and dance. Play a sport that you enjoy that increases your energy. Tennis, basketball, bicycle riding. Breathe, laugh!

If you are too wound up, relax. Slow down. Breathe. Take a bath. Get a massage, a steam or a sauna. Swim. Relax. Listen to some soothing sounds or music. Turn off the electronics. Eliminate distractions. Get outside. Sit in the garden. Take a walk. Enjoy the surroundings. Quietly, sit or lie down out there. Find a stream to sit next to or go to a relaxing beach. Take a nap. Have a cup of tea.

Get enough <u>decent</u> exercise and enough rest. Drink plenty of good, clean, pure water. Eat healthy, organic, non-processed food. Cut out sugar and too much alcohol. Savor your meal. Be with your food. IT is your nourishment. It keeps you alive. It is your fuel. Choose it wisely.

What You See Is What You Get – Visualize Only Positive Good

STOP RUSHING! Some people bless their food or ask their food to be blessed. Begin your day being grateful. Imagine it adding to your health and wellbeing. Simply eat. Enjoy tasting your food instead of reading the paper or watching media. Savor your meals. Allow the food to nourish you. No rush.

SMILE AND LAUGH MORE. Have fun. Don't MAKE PERSONAL CHANGE and transformation hard. A major tenant of Mind Design™ is to make learning and changing fun and easy Lighten up. Let go. Drop your cares and troubles, and live. Be as a child.

HAVE FUN doing and learning new things. Take some classes. Try different genres of books, music or movies. Take a spinning class or a ballroom or swing class. Make moments fun by meeting new and interesting people. Meditate or do something spiritual or natural.

He Who Enjoys Good Health Is Rich Though He Knows It Not

Have I said, spend more time outdoors? Be freer, simpler and gentler. You have work time and rest time. Learn to manage both well. The more positive your thoughts the healthier all aspects of your life can be. The healthier you are the MORE POSITIVE your thoughts can be.

Determine how you want your life to be. Claim it back. Access your power. SEE IT AND SAY HOW IT SHALL BE. Declare it and make it so. Live as a champion and an emperor, not as a victim or a pauper. Decide to live a glorious life! Make it that way minute by minute.

Change Your Feelings Checklist – Create Positive Daytime & Nighttime Rituals & Habits

1. Morning first thing before you do anything else! Count your blessings. Feel wonderful. Think, happy positive thoughts the moment you wake up! Spend 5 minutes or more setting your daytime energy right!
2. Move: Walk, skip, run, dance, Increase the variety and the intensity of your movement gently.
3. Breathe: Breathe differently. Take deep breaths
4. Get a Massage, Sauna, Acupuncture, Feldenkrais, Pamper Yourself
5. Play with a child or a pet.
6. Shift your body: Use your physiology to feel better. Walk as a wall (strong, powerful unmovable). Walk as a wire (lightly, fluidly, as if on rice paper, grasshopper!)
7. Stretch: Become more flexible.
8. Yoga, Tai Chi, Martial Arts, Aerobics, whatever form of exercise you enjoy most.
9. Use a Rebounder – a mini-trampoline. Rebound for a couple minutes numerous times a day.
10. Exercise: Swim, Water Walk, Bike, Aerobics, Crossfit, Hike,

Basketball, Tennis. Choose a sport that increases your energy.

11. Get down and roll around. Play as a little child would. Spin, Roll down a hill.
12. Take An Eye Break: About every 20 minutes or so. Look as far off as you can. Look across the room or out the window.
13. If Sitting Stand Up: Stand and walk around about every 20 minutes. Stand at your desk whenever able.
14. Walk Outdoors: Gaze far off into the distance. Look at the horizon.
15. Smile More. Laugh more. Have Fun.
16. Walk Barefoot. Connect with the earth. Lie on beach or in nature.
17. Work in the garden. Get your hands dirty.
18. Listen to music to Get Pumped Or To Relax. Music is a big one! It works for most people. Pick great music that makes you feel how you want to feel. Positive and supercharged. Positive and relaxed.
19. Meditate: Chant Mantra, Focus on your breath, many forms
20. Wound up: Relax. Breathe. Take a bath. Get a Massage, Steam, Sauna, Swim. Relax. Listen to some soothing sounds or music. Drink some relaxing tea.
21. Unplug: Turn Off the Electronics. Eliminate distractions. No Social Media or TV. Dim the lights. Get sun. No electronics 1 hour before bed.
22. Get Outside: Sit in the garden. Take a walk. Enjoy the surroundings. Quietly, sit or lie down out there. Find a stream to sit next to or go to a relaxing beach. Take a nap.
23. Laugh non-stop for 5, 10, 30 minutes. Laughter meditation. Purposefully start laughing even though you may not feel like it. Watch shows and comics that make you roar. Spend day laughing more.
24. Yawn. Breathe. Yawn. Stretch. Allow yourself to refresh and feel open and renewed. Go ahead. Yawn.

25. Get Enough Rest: Power Nap. 7-9 hours uninterrupted sleep

26. Drink plenty of good, clean, pure water. ½ body weight converted to ounces. Sipped throughout day.

27. Eat healthy, organic, non-processed food. Cut out sugar, starches, gluten, and too much alcohol. Savor your meal. Be with your food.

28. Take a spinning class or a ballroom or swing class. Learn something you have always wanted.

29. Plug In: Make each moment fun by meeting, new interesting people.

30. Help another person. Pay it forward. Give out what you wish to receive back. Smiles, good feelings, money, whatever you want back give it first. Help another feel better in whatever way you are able. Feel joy in the act of giving.

31. Forgive and Let Go when someone slights you. Release them and yourself from negative feelings. Let go. Return the slight with love and forgiveness. Create what you want instead of accepting what you don't. Make your purpose and intention is to be positive and life-giving.

32. Practice Gratitude.

33. Night Time Prior To Sleeping. Count your blessings. Journal. Write down what you are thankful for and your wins, small or large during the day. Feel grateful! Feel wonderful. Be thankful for your day and celebrate everything! Set your positive intentions for what you intend to do the next day. Go to sleep feeling wonderful. No electronics. No phone. Drift off thinking and feeling marvelous!

Put a smile on your face and then on someone else's.

CHAPTER THIRTEEN

Beliefs Determine Reality

Dion, my dear friend, was in a coma. His mother called and told me he had a 50-50 chance of coming out of it. She asked if I might visit him to see if I could help. I made arrangements and traveled to the hospital. I entered his hospital room and saw him in the bed where he had been confined for some time. I noticed personal items that were placed about around him, that his family supplied to make it feel more like home. I said hello. I spoke to him as if he were awake and able to respond.

I began commenting on the personal items placed around the room. I stated his family wanted him to be comfortable and that they provided these special things. Within a short period he opened his eyes and said 'hi'. I was stunned and elated. I knew his family desperately wanted this moment. I said, 'Stay right where you are I'll be right back!' I ran to get his family.

Upon entering the room with them, as soon as they saw him, he closed his eyes and went back inside. For a moment they realized he had been awake but no longer. From that brief, open eye moment I had with him, he went into coma and never came back out. Everyone was disappointed. I was too. I'd had him right there and had left the room. After they left the room I started to talk to him again.

I knew he could hear me. As far back as the 1970's, operating rooms in California placed signs reading, 'Careful, your patient can hear you.' I talked about important things. I said that I would like to be able to communicate with him and would it be all right to set up some signals? Then, I asked him to lift his little finger for 'yes' and to raise his forearm for 'no.' My years as a hypnotist came in handy.

Become Alert – Become Aware – There Are Infinite Possibilities

He responded favorably as I had asked. This was so cool. I asked if he liked where he was inside and he said yes. I asked if he was comfortable and he said yes. I asked if everything was OK and he said yes. I asked if he felt blissful, meditative and he said yes. A few things he did respond to with a no. It was wonderful to be able to communicate.

The hospital put a cot in another room for me to stay so this became my digs for a while. A day or two day later I was standing outside his room while doctors were inside. They were discussing him and stating that his chances were slim. They were very negative and graphic. One said it was 'shitty his insides were all screwed up.'

Upon hearing this I entered the room and asked abruptly, 'Do you think it's wise to speak about your patient when he can hear you?' Realize I'm a layperson confronting a number of god-doctors. Immediately they got snotty. 'What makes you think he can hear us?' They demanded. I said, 'because he responds.' They again asked, with even more disdain, 'and what makes you think he responds?'

I told them he responded to me. They said, 'Prove it!' Boy, did I feel on the spot. I hoped that this would work. I hoped Dion would communicate. Asking them to step out of the room I described what would take place and how he would answer. We entered the room and I began asking questions.

I asked him if he was comfortable? He indicated yes. I asked if he liked his nurses? He said, yes. I asked if he liked the doctors, his arm went up immediately in a big no. Their jaws hit the floor. They had stood mesmerized during the questioning process, but now they were beside themselves.

Your Mind Is Powerful – Fill It With Positivity

From that moment on they treated me as if I were a god. They would tell me what procedures and treatments they planned to do. I kept telling them they needed to tell his family their considerations, not me. A couple days later another new doctor entered the scene. He felt Dion was so deep in coma he couldn't respond. He would not respond to kinesthetic stimulation.

Dion remained unresponsive when pricked numerous times around his body with a pointed stick. His nurse said, 'Let's get Rex. He can communicate with Dion.' They found me. I told the doctor the signals. He conducted his test again. Each time, I would ask, 'Did you feel that?'

Dion responded correctly each time. He also said no, to the times he was asked, but not poked. This doctor was blown away too. Numerous days later, sadly, my friend died. At the time he needed and had received an organ transplant. For a short while the transplant worked and he was a new man. WOW you wouldn't believe the difference.

Then, his body went into rejection. Six weeks afterwards, the very day he returned home, he got symptoms. He went back into the hospital the very next day and soon slipped into coma. At that time, there was an experimental drug that could have been used to treat him. However, they couldn't administer the medication, by law, until they had secured positive evidence of the particular cause of the rejection he was experiencing.

They knew he was, but they couldn't find the evidence. Unable to treat him, his body and organs atrophied. All they could do was make him comfortable. Three days before he died, his main physician came to me, again circumventing the family, and said 'We've discovered the issue. We can now get permission to administer the drug.'

Joy Is A Decision – Happiness Is A Choice – Decide To Live Well

I said, 'This is great news!' He said, 'No. By the time we get the permission, it's likely he will be dead.' I was terribly disheartened. Three days later he passed. He was a dear friend and I have missed him much through the years. It was a beautiful and bittersweet time. His memorial service brought everyone to tears. He was deeply loved. I share the story for this purpose.

I believe I could communicate with him because I met him and accepted him as he was. I wasn't family hoping he'd stick around if he chose to go. I believe he was at peace about departing, based on my conversations with him. He awoke and continued to communicate with me because I paced him verbally. I met him where he was at. I completely respected him. I commented on things that he had in his room.

He knew I respected him and I would let him do whatever he chose to do. He loved his family but he also knew they wanted him to stick around. I commented on things that were important to him and that created an unconscious rapport. He was able to communicate even when most people think he should not have been. Remarkable.

Most People Miss The Obvious – Because Of The Obvious

My point is the subconscious mind is incredible. There is so much more going on than we understand. The unconscious mind can hear and does listen. It knows what's going on and pays attention; even when we are consciously distracted, it keeps track. So, it is worthwhile to learn to manage and direct your thinking to eliminate negative thoughts and distractions. Eliminate negative energy in your life wherever and whenever you are able to. Stay focused on the positive. Know that your brain works on your behalf to keep you alive.

It will do whatever it has to, good or bad, right or wrong, supportive or non-supportive, to fulfill that function. Create a wonderful relationship with yourself. Love, honor, and respect yourself.

We're Living And Growing Or Withering And Dying – Choose

We crave change but we fear it too. While our brain and body seek homeostasis and consistency, our body and brain also craves novelty and new experiences. It simply wants to keep you the same while experiencing new things. It seems contradictory, but it isn't.

We evolved to grow and change and adapt to environmental changes and dangers. The brain's job is to keep us alive. Still, it grows and evolves through play, experience, learning, challenges and obstacles. Without any challenge or resistance your muscles wouldn't grow, nor would the brain.

There are both conscious and subconscious processes at work. Therefore, BE THANKFUL for those less than glorious problems and obstacles. They force you to pay attention, so you can grow. Get it?

You Get What You Believe – Our Beliefs Shape Our Reality

When confronted with new or challenging experiences, many times, we may have consciously made excuses not to change. "Should I?" or "shouldn't I?" is an example of being stuck. Thoughts oppose each other. We feel unsure or bad, afraid to move. Why? It isn't because we think or believe something wonderful is going to happen!

We fear potential bad things. We anticipate failure. We think it will be too hard. Someone else is smarter and can do it, but 'I' can't. We have beliefs about what could go wrong and what it would mean about us if we try and fail. So, we don't try. That takes a toll on us emotionally and spiritually. It becomes part of our history data bank.

It is how we remain stuck. We perpetuate the limiting beliefs and negative feelings and wallow in them. Because we believe we can't change or make a difference, we don't. We act helpless. We don't move, nor take steps to remedy the situation.

What You Feel Is What You Get – Feel Your Best – Act As If

The remedy would be to correct the mindset to change the thoughts, beliefs, attitude and feelings that are holding you in place. This is what we should do. CHANGE YOUR THOUGHTS and thereby change the feelings, or CHANGE YOUR FEELINGS and you change the thoughts. If one does nothing, one just remains stuck.

Because people don't want to be stuck they start trying to think about how to solve the problem by fixing the situation rather than correcting the mindset it originates from. They get caught up in busy work that is less than productive. They really need to shift.

Albert Einstein pointed out, "We can't solve problems by using the same kind of thinking we used when we created them." We won't fix issues by trying to solve the issue. We need to fix the thinking. Lots of busy work, trying to remedy the situation, is less effective than a little work correcting the mindset. After all, mindset is 98% the most important.

Your Attitude Determines Your Direction And Your Altitude

Spend 98% of your time correcting your thinking and 2% of your time working on the situation. That is what Napoleon Hill meant by THINK AND GROW RICH. Work smarter not harder. Get this. It is important. You must learn where it is most important to spend your time. Actions are important. Yes! Actions are important but only after your mindset is correct!

People fear the worst but they really don't consider the worst that could happen. At times, it is a very useful and appropriate question. For example, someone thinks, "I have to pay my rent. If I don't pay my rent I will be homeless". That could be true. It is also a belief.

What they try to do is fix the money problem by working more hours, or getting another job, looking in the want ads. None of these is a bad thing to do, but what they need to fix first, is their limited thinking patterns. Once they fix that, and GET FEELING RIGHT, they will be able to think clearer and more creatively to make a difference in the situation.

Stay Positive – Be Strong – Feel Your Best – You Can Do It – Do It

Now, might be the time to ask, "What is the worst that could happen?" (See Sara's story coming up.) Obviously, she would say, "I'll be homeless." So you ask, "What is the worst that could happen?" Ask it again and again as they mentally run through all scenarios. Or, ask it of yourself. Get it?

"I won't have a place to live." "What's the worst that could happen?" "I'll end up in the gutter." "What's the worst that could happen?" "I'll become a hopeless drug addict." "What's the worst that could happen?" "I end up prostituting to get food." "What's the worst that could happen?" "I die of an overdose." Pretty dire, don't you think?

You Get What You Focus On Energy Flows Where Attention Goes

Obviously, these could either happen or not. The person may or may not even believe these will happen. The point of the asking "What is the worst that could happen," is to take it to extremes. Why, take it to extremes? Because...

These scenarios, in all likelihood, <u>will</u> <u>never</u> happen. What the person fears when they can't pay the rent is any number of things, but nothing is as bad as these things.

Still, what they fear, is keeping them stuck. It keeps them feeling bad. It will help them to put things back into perspective when they consider the worst that could happen. That's what the wealthy learn from financial disaster and bankruptcy. The worst <u>isn't</u> the worst. They go on to create riches again. Many have multiple times.

It is also a fact that most of the things we fear will happen, never do. The worst, almost <u>never</u> happens.

You Make It Happen – You Create It – You Attract It – You Do It

In a worry study conducted at Cornell University, subjects were asked to write down their worries over an extended period of time. Then, they were to report which of their imagined "worst fears" or negative circumstance did not actually happen. The results may stun you. 85% of what subjects worried about never ever happened.

Of the 15% that did occur, 79% of subjects reported they either could handle the difficulty better than they expected to, or the difficulty taught them an important lesson. This means 97% that people worry about is nothing that should stop you. Get that? 97% of worries are nothing to worry about!

Still, people live their lives feeling powerless and worried that the things they imagine happening will come to pass. Few things get really, really bad. Sometimes, yes, but far less than most of us think they do.

You're Always Out Of Your Comfort Zone If You Are Growing

Then when it comes to other changes we hope to make, we look back and find proof, from our own history of inaction, for not doing anything. We find examples when fear held us back. We find examples of when we tried and it went awry. We will find examples of when we didn't succeed, which proves us an even bigger failure. Get it. Our RAS provides us whatever we focus on and feel strongly about.

That cycle continues. Our self-image; our self-esteem; our self-confidence; our self-love eroded. We believe even worse of ourselves.

We have been conditioned to worry and spiral down. We have been conditioned to exaggerate our problems and get dramatic about them when we recount them to others. It is all habit. If we learned the habit we can learn to change it.

Stay Positive – Be Strong – Feel Your Best – You Can Do It – Do It

The purpose of Mind Design™ and this book, and the wisdom from ancient times to now from other thought leaders, is to help you feel better, and make the changes you want. My hope is that you LEAD THE LIFE YOU WANT TO LIVE. Recipes, formulas, principles and suggestions have been handed down to us for centuries so we could improve our lot. YET, few do.

By the way, this is not meant for you to stop paying your rent because of my example.

Few will improve because they don't believe anything will help. I'm going to pause here for another example. Most people fear bankruptcy? Do you? I sure did. It terrified me. Yet, I have never been bankrupt. Consider that. I feared it.

You Are Where Your Thoughts Brought You

I have known scores of people who have gone bankrupt. They are alive and are still somehow doing fine. Yes, they have changes, but none of my friends and acquaintances caused themselves harm because of it. Some people have however, and that is very sad.

Do you know what I learned about bankruptcy? I learned that bankruptcy itself teaches people, that even though it is bad, and you may be down, you are not out, and it isn't over. Every one of the bankrupt people I know, still had jobs, cars, and bought things. Some lost their homes and lived elsewhere temporarily. Most kept their homes and had money to spend. Amazing isn't it?

So while I feared going bankrupt, and still wouldn't want it, it isn't and is far from, the worst that could happen. Still people are afraid of it. People fear many different things. When people get stuck in fear and negativity they can become hopeless and helpless.

They expect help to arrive from outside of them instead of from within. The truth of the matter is inside each of us we already have what we need to live as champions, but few will look within. It is inside you where the truth resides. Remember, the truth shall set you free. LIVE AS A CHAMPION!

Many people who have been bankrupt go on to greater wealth. If you look at the lives of most wealthy entrepreneurs you'll discover many of them went flat broke. Before making their millions, they were bankrupt or on the brink of having lost everything. Many of them were far worse off than the people I previously mentioned.

Yet, they turned it around. Why? Because once they got to that extreme two things happened. One is, they didn't die. The worst wasn't as bad as they thought it might be. They learned they could eventually bounce back. So, they did.

You Make It Happen – You Create It – You Attract It – It Is You

Two, they got angry enough about their situation, that they made a final decision to get ahead. They decided to never return to poverty, but to **BECOME FINANCIALLY FREE.** They thought and exclaimed, "Never again! I WILL create wealth and that is it! Period. There is no stopping me now!" Get the attitude change?

Disaster led them to profound new insight. They learned the worst, while terrible, was still livable. They learned if they wanted to change things it was up to them. They looked within made a decision to create wealth, health, happiness or whatever. They took control of their thinking, feeling and doing to get new, different, better, positive results.

When you look within, MANAGE YOUR THOUGHTS AND BELIEFS, and feel the very best, in the face of difficulty, you learn YOU CAN HANDLE ANYTHING. You discover YOU ARE BIGGER THAN ANY OBSTACLES.

Because you win, you get better at winning. Success breeds more success, just as failure breeds more failure. When you take charge and CONTROL YOUR THOUGHTS AND FEELINGS you are driving the changes in positive directions.

What You Feel Is What You Get What You Think Is How You Feel

Instead of looking within most people are distracted. They look outside of themselves. TV, media, economy, politics, everything distracts. We look outward and outside ourselves for change. Or we look upward for help.

Everything necessary for you to begin to live the life of your dreams is already within you. In order to find it, you must first believe that is true. For some, for many, that is too big of a leap. You would be well advised, to begin by believing improvement, is at least possible. We have to create an opening in our mental armor. Our armor is fashioned by our beliefs. We wear it even when we don't need to.

Drop By Drop The Tub Fills

In order for us to change we have to, at least, entertain the possibility that it is possible to change. If we can't get this far we probably are doomed to remain stuck, standing, the same for years to come. If we can IMAGINE A BETTER DAY AHEAD we can bring it about because that which we can conceive of, and begin to BELIEVE in, we can achieve.

The reason change is difficult for some is because we look through our prison windows of beliefs. Our RAS looks for that which proves our frame of mind correct. It finds examples in the outer world to match our inner beliefs. Thankfully, though it may be tough, we can usually still find at least one reason to change.

Usually a crisis or devastating circumstance shakes us up enough to the point we wake up and exclaim, "I really need to change something here!" It is sad or unfortunate when there is a crisis, and wonderful and fortunate there is a crisis, at the same time.

Out Of Chaos Stars Are Born

If crisis is the impetus for change it is a marvelous, and bittersweet opportunity to turn your life around. It really, truly, is. I know it doesn't seem like it now, or even while going through it, at the time, but it is. Often people look back after a negative event and say something to the effect, "Wow, my life changed because of this!"

If a crisis comes and all you do is reinforce being stuck, feeling down and out, without learning something of importance from the situation, then it was an opportune time wasted. Because inside our troubles are lessons and seeds of OPPORTUNITY.

Distance Yourself From Negativity And Beautiful Things Happen

The good news is, if not now, perhaps another time. Most lessons seem to come around again and again, until we finally get it, learn something and make a change. Who knows? I don't, but it is possible another time may come.

A great state of mind to adopt is that all challenges and obstacles are blessings with hidden gifts within. Learn to celebrate everything and your life will vastly improve. Muscles grow because of resistance. Don't fight the troubles embrace them as unexpected gifts designed to help you change.

Whether or not this is actually true, the mindset is useful for making your life better. It is a needed re-frame. It is not the outer circumstances that matter as much as the meaning we assign them. Remember, we are discussing beliefs. We can re-frame anything.

Either You Run The Day Or The Day Runs You

As you read this are you aware of your agreement and disagreement? Are you aware of the beliefs you have around the points I am making? If you BECOME MORE AWARE of what you think and believe, congratulate yourself. Not everyone will reflect in this fashion. It is a very useful exercise and a good way to spend your time. Examine your beliefs.

How are you doing on remaining open and available to learn new things? Are you able to try on different points of view and new beliefs? I ask because I am curious? Plus, it matters how open you are to learning and to changing. Remember, the teacup story? You have to **MAKE ROOM TO INCLUDE NEW THINGS.** Remember, the three most dangerous words? Get it?

Continue the process of looking for and finding those beliefs that support you and enable you, and those that don't. What does having those beliefs mean about you? You can ask this question of each belief you discover. Examine and reflect on it. Write it down.

Be Willing To Explore

Hang loose with whatever answer you get. It is just another belief. Still, discover the supportive ones that make you feel your best and enhance and amplify those. Promote what you want. This is a golden key. **REINFORCE THE GOOD** and the positive that supports you.

Diminish and let go of the ones that don't serve you. Drop the ones you don't want. Really <u>learn</u> this! <u>You</u> choose! You are in charge! When <u>you</u> take control **YOU DECIDE** which beliefs you will let influence you and which will not.

You begin to live from the powerful supportive beliefs that serve you and you start thriving. This is so cool. You get back more of what you put out. You choose strong positive beliefs and feelings and you end up creating more of the same.

All Things Are Difficult Before They Are Easy

If you encounter a challenge or some limiting beliefs arise in the future, and they will, <u>you</u> <u>are</u> <u>equipped</u> to handle them and keep your life on track, without getting derailed. **YOU ARE IN CHARGE.**

Any time you attempt something new or there is a life change, other beliefs come up, you thought you had eliminated. **THIS IS A GREAT THING.** Celebrate. It is as if you are searching a dark room with a flashlight. These events illuminate those remaining beliefs. Examine each.

As a result, you have the opportunity to transform them. Obstacles and problems provide us the opportunity to shift to the positive, let go of the negative and feel more wonderful. Recognize troubles for the blessings they are and your life and abilities will excel.

What You Think About Most Often You Become

Exercise: Watch your thoughts. Observe them. Notice each one you become aware of. Your feelings will be your guide. Within these pages you have been learning to ask yourself, "what do I want?" You have been learning to shift from what you do not want to what you do want. You are learning to shift from the negative, non-supportive thoughts and habits to positive, supportive ones. You are becoming aware.

Plus, you are using that awareness to instigate change. Another extremely powerful question to ask is "Do I want this thought?" Since birds of a feather flock together, and one thought attracts another like or similar thought, you only want to attract the best ones. You want to perpetuate the most positive, powerful, wonderful, high vibration thoughts possible, and let go of, drop and eliminate those others.

Ask yourself, "Is this the kind of thought I want more of?" If not, change it to one you do want more of and focus on the new thought for a while. Spend time concentrating on this new thought you do want. Spend less time giving any attention to thoughts you don't want. Get it? Nurture and encourage what you want more of. Starve what you want less of. It is simple in principle. Learn to do it. This is powerful!

What You Think And Say Is What You Get – Believing Is Seeing

When you find a thought that you want more of, that makes you feel wonderful, energized, freer, filled with joy, write it down. Talk about it.

Think on it frequently. Accentuate, enhance and amplify it. Repeat it. Use it to attract more of the same thoughts. Increase the flow of positive thought energy. You do it by deliberately encouraging and focusing on it. Remember, we become what we think about most of the day.

What we think about expands. So expand only what you want. If it feels good and positive, do more of it. If it feels less than glorious, do less of it. Your feelings will always be your guide. You must deliberately, consciously make the choices and the change. As you do it becomes easier and easier. You begin attracting more positive thoughts and wonderful feelings into your life. You outer world changes too!

Recognize beliefs for what they are, mental packets of energy, in clusters. These belief clusters shape your view of the world. They either enable or disable you from moving forward. Either they are supportive or not. Whenever they arise, have the courage and tenacity to examine, challenge and re-frame them for your benefit. Make your beliefs work for you, instead of against you. "Do I want this thought?"

Whether You Think You Can Or You Can't You're Right

Keep in mind one of your main goals is to feel good most of the time. Legally, good, I might add. Only do those things that are positive and good for you and everyone else. Still, the point is to maximize the time you feel good and minimize the less than glorious feelings. You change your thoughts and you change your feelings to spend more time feeling wonderful because that creates more of the same. Get it?

Soon, you have developed a momentum for thinking and feeling wonderful. You begin to intuitively take the right actions, find yourself in the right places, with the right people who are good for you to know and associate with. You begin creating and attracting more of what you want. As you do, you feel more inspired, more thrilled, more passionate and wonderful. As you feel these you begin to get more of them.

Life becomes an incredible and awesome adventure. You begin creating and attracting more of what you want in life. Remember the more you win the easier it becomes to continue winning. You begin to develop a habit of thinking and feeling good and you begin discovering yourself automatically feeling magnificent. When trying times come your way you respond more resourcefully from your new habits!

Birds Of A Feather Flock Together – Like Attracts Like

Exercise: When facing difficult times be willing to consider "What is the worst that could happen?" Ask it often, again and again. Write down each answer you receive. As you get answers, realize and recognize that most of the scenarios are not likely. However, if one is, that is useful information to know.

Write down your answers as you go through this process. Analyze them. Evaluate whether these 'believed' scenarios help you, or prevent you, in getting what you want. FOCUS ON THE POSITIVE, supportive beliefs and ideas you get, that help you MOVE FORWARD IN POSITIVE WAYS.

The goal of the exercise is to get unstuck in your thinking by shining the flashlight of consciousness on your thinking. How has it been stopping or preventing you? You can ask yourself this question too, and write down the answer.

Energy Isn't Created Or Destroyed – Energy Is Transformed

How realistic are the fears, you have feared? Ask and write down the answer. Drop the ones that keep you stuck and don't serve you. Shift and FOCUS ON THE ONES THAT ENABLE AND SUPPORT YOU. Lastly, make sure what you want is positive for you and positive for all the people involved.

Write down your answers. Look for those beliefs that support you and enable you, and those that don't. What does having those beliefs mean about you? Ask and write down the answer. You can ask this question of each belief you discover. Examine and reflect and write down the answers.

It takes some courage, patience and persistence to want to uncover your thoughts and beliefs. That is just the way it is. Remember, if you think YOU CAN or you think you can't, you are right. Keep examining your beliefs. Changing your beliefs will put you on the path toward making the life you want come true.

Enjoy and delight in your day!

"Your inner strength is your outer foundation."
— *Allan Rufus*

"Please don't ever think that you can't get out of the rut you may be in or think you can't take your life to a whole new level. Anything is possible when you have a path, a plan and a desire to take action."
— *Dean Graziosi*

"Love yourself enough to take the actions required for your happiness; love yourself enough to cut yourself loose from the ties of the drama filled past; love yourself enough to move on."
— *Dr. Steve Maraboli*

"No amount of reading or memorizing will make you successful in life. It is the understanding and application of wise thought which counts."
— *Bob Proctor*

"We are shaped by our thoughts; we become what we think. When the mind is pure, joy follows like a shadow that never leaves."
— *Buddha*

CHAPTER FOURTEEN

The Success Formula Laid Bare

Some people struggle. They try everything but get almost nowhere. Or it seems they go backwards. Others seem to work hard and get ahead. Some seem to skyrocket to success. What gives? Why do some make it and others don't?

Some try many things. Some try the Law Of Attraction. Perhaps, you have. You tried some things but you end up in the same condition, or even worse. Have you had difficulty getting the LOA to work?

Some people have incredible success with the LOA. Here is why. The answer is quite simple, although you may not like it.

What You See Is What You Get

When it comes to the Law Of Attraction I don't rule anything out. I think most people have trouble because they think fancifully instead of powerfully. They think of it as rubbing the genie's lamp. It is not the same.

The LOA is based on the notion that like attracts like. Whatever thoughts or energy you put out there; whatever you think or 'vibrate' at you get more of the same back. Birds of a feather flock together. Like attracts like. What goes around comes around. Get it? You get more of the same.

People think, "Okay, I want more happiness." "I want more love." "I want more money." They think: "More happiness." "More Love.' 'More money." But nothing happens. They get a little frustrated and try to think harder. "More happiness!" "More happiness!!" "More love!" "More love!!" "More money!" "More money!!" On it goes. They get louder!

The reason it isn't working is that it IS working. HUH? It IS working? You are getting back what you are thinking about or vibrating at.

If You Want All Things To Change Faster – Change Yourself

You exclaim, "Wait no, no I am not. I haven't, I tried it. Now, I am frustrated. I want more of these things and I haven't got them yet." Exactly! That is the truth. You want more and you haven't got them yet. You are frustrated.

You are struggling with it and the LOA is bringing back to you more of what you are putting out there. You are getting struggle, frustration, impatience, and lack. You are getting more of the same!

You are getting back the lack of what you notice is missing. If you are thinking, "I want this," it means you don't have it yet. If you notice not having it, you are noticing the lack of it. Hence, what you vibrate is the lack of having. Congratulations! You are attracting more lack, back. You are getting what you put out, which is more of the same.

What You Say Is What You Get

See, you don't attract what you want. You attract, and get back, what you are, and who you are. This is the incredible secret point most people miss and the mistake they make.

People think it is the words that make a difference. "I want money". It isn't the words but the feeling surrounding the thought. If you desperately want money you are desperate. If you want money because you are in debt, you are feeling lack and debt. Get it? You are feeling, emitting or vibrating the opposite of what you want.

If you want more happiness you must first BE HAPPINESS! If you want more love, you must BE LOVE first. If you want more money you must put money out there first. You attract like things! You attract what you currently, and already, are! If YOU ARE HAPPI-NESS, you will get more happiness back!

Life Isn't What Happens To You – Life Is What You Create

The Law Of Cause And Effect states that "For every cause there will be an equal and opposite effect". What you initiate, you will get back. These laws work together, not in isolation. This is why you get back what you are and not what you want. This is important to understand!

What you want, you do not, yet, have. What you are is right now. You get back more of what is right now. So, if what is right now, you are broke, you get more broke back. If what is right now, you are lonely, you get more lonely back. You get back what is.

A magnet attracts another magnet or piece of metal not some imaginary future magnet or piece of metal. Do you get this, yet? If you want something NOW you must BE IT now. That is why mindset is so important!

What You Feel Is What You Get

This is why wishing, hoping, praying, begging, bargaining and threatening doesn't work. When you do any of these you are coming from a place of lack. You are not what you want to attract. And so you attract not what you want.

If you want happiness you must first BECOME HAPPINESS. You must think it, feel it, act it and live it. You must be it. You declare it already into being. You 'act as if' it is right here, right now, even when it isn't yet. You imagine the good you want as already happened.

You imagine it. Relate to it 'as if' you have already accomplished it. You live in the reality you want to live in before actually getting there. From this place you attract the same. This is how you

VIBRATE HAPPINESS. You THINK AND FEEL HAPPY. Then you create and attract happy.

What You Are Is What You Get

You attract what you already are. If you want more money act like you already have more money. LIVE IT, breathe it and enjoy it. Give it. You can't be worried about making ends meet and financially free at the same time. Even if the bank account is low you need to celebrate!

Every time you pay a bill you need to think "Good thing I am rich." Or, "I love circulating money." Or, "Every dollar that flows out comes back to me multiplied." That is how you attract more. You won't attract it if you tighten the belt and think, "I am running out of cash."

Mindset comes first. It begins WITHIN YOU, before you get the results in the outer world. You have to have the correct thoughts and feelings and actions in place first. When you have the mindset of someone wealthy, then you attract more of the same!

Attitude Determines Your Altitude

Right now, you are already attracting more of the same! It just isn't what you want. You tried visualizing, etc., and claim it doesn't work. Actually, it works too well! You are getting what you are already thinking about.

If you think it doesn't work, congratulations! It won't. People constantly affirm lack, thinking they are affirming prosperity. They aren't. They stay broke and claim they aren't attracting anything. They are! They are attracting, staying broke. Do you get this?

Your thoughts determine your reality! If your thoughts are positive and powerful, happy, about abundance, joyful and grateful, you feel that way. When you feel that way, you do things differently than when you are bummed out.

Take Action Steps

You attract more good feelings from those good feelings. Like attracts like. That is why successful people with money seem to make more money. It seems to come to them with ease. Well, it does, because they think wealthy and successfully.

If your results suck it means your thinking sucks! Sorry, but it is true. You have to examine your thinking and get right with your thoughts first. They can't be half positive and half negative. They can't be mostly negative. Most people never get this.

Either you are thinking decrease or increase. If you want increase you must be increase. Think increase, feel increase, speak increase, and behave increase. YOU MUST BE IT! When YOU ARE IT you GET MORE OF IT! You attract likeness!

What You Think About You Bring About

People keep missing this. They blame themselves, others, and they look for missing secrets. They try all sorts of things. They don't have to. They only have to get this one area correct. This is what unleashes the positive changes! Attitude determines your altitude.

Some want to sit around and imagine checks appearing out of thin air. If you sit in a room and hope they will manifest by meditating day and night, good luck. I won't rule it out, but that alone, isn't likely. However, I believe anything is possible.

If you are active in your mind, if your thinking is corrected first, and you are out working your plan and creating the life you want, because your attitude is right, you can see a nice payoff from many places. It works. It may be surprising and seem to come from thin air like magic. But it isn't. You made it happen.

Money comes quickly to those who succeed because once at the top everyone else wants a piece of the successful person. Checks can begin to 'just' show up. BUT it didn't happen by rubbing a lamp or meditating on dollars flowing to you. It comes because <u>you</u> <u>are</u> <u>successful</u>!

Now, here is an important point. Meditating on money flowing to you <u>can</u> be useful. Meditating on money <u>is</u> foundational work. You begin to ADOPT THE RIGHT MINDSET by imagining money flowing in. IMAGINE YOU ARE WORTHY, imagine you **already** have money <u>and</u> it feels good.

From Within To Without

In this case it is not wishful thinking. Meditating on dollars flowing to you is a great way to begin to get your mindset right. You begin to <u>see</u> <u>yourself</u> <u>as</u> <u>one</u> <u>who</u> attracts money, or as a vessel for cash, or a conduit for abundance. You begin to relate to money positively.

That is great. That is preliminary work to get your mindset right. You deserve wealth. You absolutely want to meditate and get the right attitude. That is the important <u>first</u> step. You have to FEEL WEALTHY. FEEL ABUNDANCE! FEEL YOU DESERVE IT. Feel it come to you.

Then take it further. It isn't just coming to you. YOU are making it happen. Imagine already having it. Imagine being successful. Imagine how you got it legally and ethically. Enjoy! Live the dream in your mind. FEEL ALL THE MARVELOUS FEELINGS.

It Is Important To Be Able To Give And To Be Able To Receive

Eventually, you must develop a plan for getting it. You won't get it sitting in your room. You must act. You don't have to know 'the how' at the start, but you will down the road. In time, it will come to you.

Because you think on it day and night, and maintain a positive frame of mind, your <u>subconscious</u> puts together an action plan. Your brain literally looks for matches within your experiences and in

REX STEVEN SIKES

your outer world. It pulls together your resources. YOUR BRAIN WORKS ON IT for you. Remember this?

The subconscious mind doesn't know the difference between an internal, made up visualization and the real world. Whatever internal representation you have made is what your brain assumes is true and acts on.

If you are broke, unhappy and lonely your brain is operating off those internal images, thoughts, and feelings. That is why you keep getting more of the same. Whatever you say you have is what you will have. What you see is what you get. Do you understand?

Your Brain, Your Mind, Your Subconscious Is Really Your Friend

This is an important point. If you don't have the results you want, you aren't thinking and imagining the results, as they will be. You are stuck imagining them as they currently are. You are looking at your outer circumstances and noting 'nothing has changed'. So it won't!

This is why Napoleon Hill said 'Think and grow rich'. It starts with thinking. Get your thinking right and you can grow rich! YOU CAN BE, DO OR HAVE ANYTHING YOU WANT. He stated you first need to be able to conceive what you want and believe it. Then you can achieve it.

Your Brain Is The Workhorse, You Are The Director

BECOME IT and you can have it! You will attract what you are because that is already what you are doing. You are already getting what you are ON THE INSIDE. If you don't like what you have been getting, you can CHANGE IT! That is the fantastic news. Awareness is the first part of transformation.

Understand why and how you have been getting less than glorious results. Then change your thoughts. Take control. Put yourself in charge. Think positively and act powerfully to become what it is you want to attract. You <u>can</u>, if you apply yourself. Might it take some time? YES!

If you are overweight by 25 or 50 pounds you know THAT didn't happen overnight. It took time to get there. You should expect it to take some time to return to your normal and ideal weight. It will take some time to learn to attract what you want. You must be okay with this. If you aren't, you'll just attract more of whatever the issue is. STOP IT!

You Already Have Everything You Need For Transformation

The way to change is to be positive. Have fun! DELIGHT! FEEL JOYFUL MOST OF THE TIME. EVOLVE YOURSELF. It won't happen to you, but <u>you</u> <u>make</u> it happen. How? By developing the right attitude. Become what you want to have more of, and you will! Live in appreciation. FEEL GRATITUDE! Celebrate everything!

What makes you feel thrilled?

"Outside of physics and the rule of law, all other rules are illusions that we've chosen to believe. Smash the ones that no longer serve you."
— *Vishen Lakhiani*

"Anger, resentment and jealousy doesn't change the heart of others. It only changes yours."
— *Sharon L. Alder*

"If you don't have some self-doubts and fears when you pursue a dream, then you haven't dreamed big enough."
— *Joe Vitale*

"Fears about money inhibit your wealth attraction powers. Absence of fears about money releases your full wealth attraction power."
— *Dan Kennedy*

CHAPTER FIFTEEN

Don't Make Your Life About Solving Problems

Life is just too short, don't you think? Why spend it locked fighting obstacles and problems? As already stated, numerous times, what you focus on is what you find! What you focus on is what you get. So focus on the good in life.

FOCUS ON OPPORTUNITIES. Focus on what you can do. Focus on who and what you love. Focus on delight and abundance. What you think about you bring about. What you focus on literally expands.

Remember, your brain looks for matches within you and your experience, and outside of you in your circumstances, based on what you are concentrating on, or holding in your mind. Energy flows where your attention goes. FOCUS ON CREATING THE BEST LIFE you can have, so you can begin to start having that.

It Is Believing Is Seeing And Not The Other Way Around

I keep repeating some of this because I want to drive home these important points. Repetition, consistently over time creates habits. I want to constantly expose your mind to key principles so you lock them in and utilize them. I want you to develop positive thought habits. Reading this book over and over will help you tremendously.

FOCUS ON LOVE and not hate. Focus on happiness, not sadness. Focus on health, not disease. Focus on wealth, not on lack. Focus on peace, not on war. Focus on gratitude and celebration and you will get more of the same. Whatever you focus on, you will get more back. You become what you think about.

If you focus on problems and obstacles that is what you will find. Don't ignore them. Handle them swiftly. Do whatever needs to be done and then <u>shift</u> your thinking back over to your goal and what you want.

Smile And Laugh Make All Of Life Beautiful

Handle the situations and <u>re-aim</u> your mind. Do not make you life about handling or solving problems. The trouble for most people is they are always 'dealing' with things. It's always one thing after the other. Their focus is on what is going wrong, not on what is going right.

Their focus is on what they don't have, not what they do have. If you want things to go right you <u>must</u> think about things going right. This is how it all works. It is very simple.

Yet most people spend 98% of their time doing busy things trying to remedy the situation and only 2%, if that, on their mindset. You need to reverse this. 98% <u>should</u> <u>be</u> <u>mindset</u> work and <u>2%</u> doing the right <u>actions</u>. Right action, comes from right mindset. Not the other way around.

What You Focus On Expands

If you want to be wealthy think about, focus on, making, investing and growing your money. Focus on keeping your money. Stop focusing on spending it, the bills, and on not having enough. Stop actually spending it. Remember, your brain looks for matches. It is a faithful servant! <u>Stop</u> looking for what is wrong. Look for opportunities.

The difference between happy, successful, rich people and those who aren't is most often, simply this. The happy, successful, rich people focus on what they want. Those who are unhappy, not successful and broke, focus on what they do not want. The happy and successful fraternize with other happy and successful people. Those who aren't fraternize with other broke and unhappy people.

The unsuccessful miss opportunities because their minds aren't tuned in for them. If you are focused on problems and troubles you are missing many opportunities because, the matches your brain finds are more of the same troubles. If you want opportunities, you have to BE FOCUSED ON THE GOOD THINGS the brain would look for.

Stop Wasting Time With Small And Large Distractions

Henry Ford, the man who said, "Whether you think you can or you think you can't, you are right," also said. "I think about what I can do. I put my attention on what I can do in any situation and what I can't do falls away." He doesn't waste time with what he cannot do! Think and speak only to bless, heal and prosper. Think what you CAN DO! Focus solely on what you can and will do. Focus on the positive!

Stop wasting time with petty distractions. Social media, gossips, arguments, bad news, it is filled with plenty of things to let go of. Start filling your mind, heart and being with good things and inspiring messages. Surround yourself with positive, inspiring, motivating people and you will have more of the same. The more you do these things the further ahead you will travel quickly. If you don't, you won't.

A negative attitude never makes for a positive life. Life is too short to be caught up in what is wrong. You can make it right. YOU CAN CHANGE THINGS. You can change your mindset and alter your circumstances. You can be, do and have whatever you want, when you start believing you can and that you deserve it.

Live Your Purpose You Deserve To

After all, aren't you worth all the joy and happiness in life? Aren't you worth all the love, family and friendship? If you aren't convinced of this you have work to do on changing some limiting beliefs.

I encourage you to stop and MAKE THOSE CHANGES NOW, so you can embrace being worthy of all the abundance, joy, love and happiness in life. Get it? Do it! Go back and repeat the exercises we have done so far. Do them daily!

You've been born into an abundant universe. You can have all that you want without depriving anyone else of their share, too. Focus on creating what you want to include more of. Exclude the rest. You can do this!

Take Charge Of Yourself – Decide To Make The Day Marvelous

Make it a point to SHIFT YOUR THINKING. Begin to LIVE THE LIFE YOU DESERVE. You can. You absolutely can! Don't put it off. Begin today. Focus your mind on what you want. Use it to bring you more of the good things in life.

You mind is your faithful servant when aimed properly. Whatever you focus on it will bring you more of. Take the energy away from what you do not want. Put that energy into what you do want. Enjoy more of life. CELEBRATE EVERYTHING!

Exercise: To develop your concentration. Get a battery operated tealight candle. It is safer than a real candle. Dim the lights. Be comfortably seated. Place the tealight on a table or surface in front of you. Lightly gaze at the tealight. Keep your focus and concentration on the light. Whenever you notice you attention wandering bring it back to the tealight.

Stay with this for ten minutes. Gradually you can increase the duration. The goal is to watch the tealight without other thought distractions. Gently, shift back to the light whenever you notice yourself drifting into other thoughts. One benefit is you develop your power to concentrate and stick with it.

Mastery Is A Process – It Takes As Much Time As It Takes – Enjoy

Exercise: Whenever you become aware of being less than glorious in your thoughts or speech, STOP and take a breath. Create a momentary pause and then change the thought or speech to a positive, supportive, statement or belief. Whatever thought or negative statement you had, rephrase it in the positive.

AFFIRM WHAT YOU WANT. Let go of what you don't want. "I don't want to be broke." Stop! Breathe! Change It! "I want to be wealthy" to "I am wealthy" or "I am learning to enjoy greater wealth." Stop affirming what you don't want. Only, affirm what you prefer.

Train your mind to drop the negativity. Replace it with positivity. FOCUS ON REMAINING POSITIVE and condition yourself to THINK POSITIVE MORE OFTEN. The benefit is you become more aware of limiting beliefs and statements and then automatically change them into supportive ones.

Your Attitude Determines Your Altitude

Keep this in mind. Think and SPEAK ONLY TO BLESS, HEAL AND PROSPER YOURSELF AND OTHERS. Put a guard before you mind and lips. Don't talk about what you don't want. Don't give that any energy at all. Stop talking about, and thinking about, and putting energy into, what you don't want! Stop telling your negative stories of woe. Just stop it! Control yourself! Take charge.

Break the negative, non-supportive habit! Manage yourself. Condition yourself to speak only that which supports you. Think and talk about your wins, and your successes. Promote what you do want. Let go of what you don't want. Withdraw from all negative, or less than glorious energy. Stop giving it attention.

Put your attention where it serves and supports you. Use some discipline. You can do this. Just do it! Begin now. Don't wait. Do it today.

Make the decision and commit to it. Then, keep your commitment. Persist! Only think and speak of what you do want and what you want to create. See it, feel it, speak it. Get it? When you do this you are on your way to making life so much better. Create your best life!

Delight in this day!

CHAPTER SIXTEEN

Isn't It Time To Be The Person You Always Wanted To Be?

You have read this far already. Isn't it time to be the person you always wanted to be? If you want to BE MORE SUCCESSFUL and happier, and BE THE PERSON YOU DREAMED you can be, then you must make some new decisions. YOU MUST DECIDE, to choose, how you want to think, feel, act and live your life.

Sara found herself in a dark abyss. She was free-spirited and had a love of all people, cultures and adventure but things did not turn out well. Things got bad. She got addicted to heroin. To feed her habit she worked as an escort. Things got worse. She became a street prostitute and a crack addict. As bad as it was, she loved the street life.

During her upbringing no one ever told her she had potential as a human being. She came from a long line of struggling people, riddled with alcoholism and depression. Yet, she now believes sinking to the bottom and surviving that homeless street life, gave her the knowledge and confidence to tap into her true potential. It was a blessing in disguise.

From The Bottom To The Top

In 1996 at twenty-six, she became pregnant by a Dominican man, who dealt in large levels of cocaine and distributed heroin. Early in the pregnancy she discovered he was using her as a drug mule. She knew she had to get out. She had to change her life! She left him.

Fortunately, at this horrible low point, she reached out. As bad as it got she sought help. She knew she needed support to change her life. So she reached out to a friend who was there for her. Her mom. Her mother determined to help her make a good life.

Sara wanted to stop hurting herself. She knew she had to make better choices. She decided she wanted to live a life of her own design. Sara made a commitment to meditation. She dove into Buddhist practices. She has not looked back since. Sara changed her mindset.

Give Yourself Permission To Change For The Better

She transformed. Since that time she has raised two amazing daughters. Her girls are beautiful human beings. Sarah left the gutter and became a productive member of society. She worked herself out of the gutter to incredible success. She's now a well-respected community leader. As a business owner and real estate investor, Sara is in the top ten percent of her industry.

Besides her house in New York she owns a second beachfront home in the Caribbean. She is an ordained Buddhist priest and teacher. Most importantly, she is a happy, positive person. Sara has no regrets and is grateful for her journey.

If you don't decide now, you are living from a past decision. If that is fine with you, then carry on. If, however, you wish things were different, you want to GET BETTER RESULTS, you don't like your present circumstances, if this is how you think and feel, then you must MAKE A NEW DECISION.

Stay Loyal To What You Said After Your Mood Has Changed

You must take the bull by the horns and CHOOSE TO CHANGE THINGS in your life that will enable you to MAKE A DIFFER-ENCE for yourself. If you don't decide, someone else chooses for you, perhaps recently, perhaps a long time ago, when you were very young. Still, someone chose for you. You need to make your own decisions. Don't live from the past.

If you don't act in your own best interest now, today, in the present, some other decision, made by some other person, is controlling you and your outcomes. You may not even realize you have adopted this decision from someone else. If you are okay with that, carry on. If not, CHANGE IT NOW. You are the only one who should be in charge of yourself and your destiny. You need to BE IN CONTROL.

Decide to be different. You may say, "Wait you don't understand, it is not that easy". I understand it is not easy and that it COULD be easy.

Your Future Does Not Depend On Your Past

Whatever you think it is, is what it will be. If you think it is hard, you will be correct. If you THINK IT EASY, you will be right then, too.

Your thoughts make it so. Whatever you focus on expands.

Your thoughts determine what you get. Your thoughts create your feelings. Your feelings lead to your actions, what you do or what you don't do. Your actions lead to the results you get.

Stand By Your Word Don't Give It If You Aren't True To It

The starting point for all the results is your thoughts. If you don't like the results you have been getting, then you need to change your thoughts. START NOW.

Give yourself permission. Make it okay for yourself to think and feel differently. Give yourself permission to see and feel and act differently, to get different, better, positive, and more powerful results.

Give yourself permission to CHANGE YOUR LIFE for the better. GIVE YOURSELF PERMISSION to make a new decision. Allow it. PERMIT IT. Accept it.

From Doctor To Artist

Ever since Tommy was a young child his mother drilled into his head that he would become a doctor. She provided him a privileged and comfortable life while they focused on making this his profession. In college he stumbled onto art, singing and acting. He fell in love with it. Nonetheless he graduated with a degree in biology.

After college he returned home and lived with his mother but had no heart for medicine. Their worst fight over it ended with his departure from her house. He didn't want others to dictate his life any longer. He turned his back on his old comfortable one.

He ended up homeless. All he had was his car and a laptop computer. Living without a home and a regular job allowed him to figure out what was truly necessary in his life. He thought about the steps he'd need to take on his new life path. He was an actor but there is little demand for another one. So he decided to pursue filmmaking.

Life Will Never Change Until You Change Something

He moved to a new city, to study film at the University. He also took up martial arts. He found it ironic that such a violent activity taught him a great deal about art and its relation to the human experience. Martial arts, is not like other sports.

Anybody can LEARN IT AND BENEFIT. It doesn't require any special talents or athleticism. All that is required is the same mindset and dedication one uses to LIVE SUCCESSFULLY. He discovered that being a good martial artist is more than the successful execution of offensive and defensive movements.

Rather, it is someone who can make a plethora of good decisions. From boxing, he learned there are different ways to stand when doing nothing. These stances mean he has different methods of attack and defense. He can string any combination of attacks and defenses together, multiplying the total number of possible actions he can take.

To Change Your Life You Have To Change Yourself

That's with just hands alone. The possibilities grow exponentially when he adds in kicks and wrestling. Once the options are figured out, all that is left is to decide what to do. He correlates this with art. He sees martial arts and art as a series of decisions.

Tommy says; "If I were to paint a picture, I must first DECIDE on a canvas, its shape, its color, and its size. Then I must decide what I want to paint, which is only limited by the human imagination. Then I must decide how to paint, what type of paint to use, what color of paint, and where each brush stroke should go."

The same is true for music, dance, writing, and filmmaking. In the end, is that not what life is? Art is a celebration of life itself. We are who we choose to be. People who live their lives making excuses for inaction and indecision will never understand this. It is not our wishes or dreams that MAKE LIFE MEANINGFUL, but rather our decisions.

Your Future Depends On The Decisions You Make Today

People want things to CHANGE FOR THE BETTER and get frustrated when they don't. Things will remain the same, as long as you remain the same. As long as you act from the past, you will continue to get what you have always got. Move into the present. Decide now to make it different. GIVE YOURSELF PERMIS-SION, to use and ENJOY YOUR PRESENT, to create a more wonderful future.

Some people never change because they don't feel it is okay that they do. They remain stuck. You may need to give yourself permission and that is fine. Go ahead. Acknowledge that it is okay for you to MOVE FORWARD. It's okay to CHANGE POSITIVELY. Allow yourself to be okay with the unknown. The future is wide open.

You can accomplish many things in the future once you get beyond being stuck. What keeps someone stuck is mostly old, chronic conditioning. That's okay it served you for a time and now it is time to change, let go, and move forward in a positive direction of YOUR choosing. Permit yourself to BE FREE OF THE PAST. Take charge now. When you do, it can begin to FEEL INCREDIBLE. Enjoy it.

To Change Yourself You Must Change Your Thought Habits

Exercise: Write down who you are and who you want to be. Write down the qualities, values and beliefs, characteristics and attributes of the new improved you. What do you embody? What is important to you? How do you think, speak, act and behave? What kind of person are you? Be thorough and exhaustive.

Write down what you want to do. What career, hobbies, vacation, fun, and leisure things do you want? Write down what you'd like to learn to do; sew, play piano, invest your money, sculpt, and so on. Make it your bucket list of activities. Be thorough and exhaustive.

Write down those things you want to have. List items, a watch, clothes, cars, a new home, and more. Whatever it is you desire. Be thorough and exhaustive.

Life Is Much Better When We Realize We Don't Know Everything

What is important to you? In general terms, what is most important to you? Then be specific. Be thorough and exhaustive.

What about attracting a positive relationship? Write down the characteristics and inner and outer attributes of your relational partner. What is important to that person? Who are they (not a specific person) but who are they as a person? What do they do? What is important to them? How do they treat others and go through the world? What do you want your ideal person to be? Be thorough and exhaustive.

With family and friends write down all you appreciate about each of them. Validate and find all the good things. Focus on these. Be grateful you have these people in your life. Be thorough and exhaustive.

Create your list. Choose one area, one thing to focus on and manifest. Use what you have been learning. 1. Visualize it in vivid detail. 2. Affirm it enthusiastically with positive strong feelings. 3. Feel good about it. If you don't feel great about thinking of it as already yours adjust it until you do.

Otherwise, choose another one you already feel eager and excited and good about. 4. Celebrate already having it. 5. Let go and trust you will make it happen. BELIEVE IN YOURSELF. Become certain. Have fun with this. Take it lightly and do it daily. Frequently. Imagine what it is like to already have what you desire. ENJOY FEELING POSITIVE! Feel good about moving forward. Enjoy this thoroughly.

Insanity Is Doing The Same Thing Expecting It To Be Different

I hope you wrote down everything you could think of when you did the exercise. Repeat it, often. Get clear about what is important to you and what you want. Enjoy realizing this is the beginning. Many new ways of being can open up to you. Now do it again, with this thought in mind. If money wasn't an object, what would you be, do and have? Do your wants change? If yes, do this exercise thoroughly now!

Are you dreaming big enough? Perhaps, you dream too small? If money didn't matter, perhaps you'd cure all disease in the world, feed all the starving nations, launch a satellite or buy an island? What would you be, do and have if money were unlimited? Imagine, think, dream, wish, and discover what you would do if money were not an object at all. Be thorough and exhaustive.

When finished pick something to focus on. Go through the steps previously listed. Make sure that whatever you do, that you feel wonderful. You feel good when you think about it. If you can't keep feeling great when you entertain it, choose something smaller that is a first step in getting you there. Something you believe you can get and feel good about!

DO this exercise frequently. Focus on what you want. Build your life. Design it. Include things you may never have considered before. Make it rich, lavish and luxurious. You deserve it. Get it? Decide what you want to go for and go for it. Remember, aim for the stars!

If you fall short and hit the moon you still went further than you might otherwise have! Aim high. Think big and make your dreams come true. Isn't it time to be the person you always wanted to be? Do those things you always wanted to do. Have those things you have always wanted.

You Get What You Focus On – What You Focus On Expands

Isn't it time for you to begin today? BEGIN RIGHT NOW!

Delight and celebrate everything!

"An inability to release negative emotions from the past is like trying to drive by using only your rearview mirror. You can't pivot by looking backward."
—— Adam Markel

"If you want to change the fruit, you have to change the roots. If you want to change the visible, you have to change the invisible first."
—— T. Harv Eker

"Life is a series of decisions that cuts off infinite possibilities at every turn. Most people look at that as a sad unfortunate fact of life. Successful people see it as a source of tremendous power."
—— Mark Joyner

CHAPTER SEVENTEEN

Use Your Attention For Success And Happiness

Napoleon Hill wrote that definiteness of purpose is the starting point of all achievement. Without a Definite Chief Purpose (DCP) or a Definite Chief Aim (DCA) and a plan, people will drift aimlessly through life. Your Definite Chief Purpose is the most important and necessary beginning element!

I talked about this before. You've encountered this idea many times already in this book. Now, it is time for you to TAKE ACTION on it.

When asked, many people say they don't know what they want. These people just can't make much happen, even though they would like and want to. They can't because they have no clear picture or idea of what it is they do want. You can't aim at a target if you don't know what it is.

Energy Goes Where Attention Goes – Focus On What You Want

You will drift around if you don't know your destination. Imagine taking a trip and not knowing where you are going. While it can be an exciting adventure, you are really only sightseeing. If you know where you want to end up, the final city, you know whether you are getting closer or not.

This is why you must know what you want! You must BE CLEAR about your Definite Chief Purpose. Why are you here? What is your big PURPOSE IN LIFE? What do you want most and feel most passionate about?

Exercise: Write down the answers to those and this next question. If you could do anything at all, and money didn't matter, what would you do for your life? If you are unsure, consider the opposite. What are you not here for? What isn't your purpose in life? What do you not want most? Get it?

It can help you to recognize what you do want by determining what you don't want. It provides contrast. Contrast is the opposite; hot, cold, light, dark, big, small, in, out and more. So if you have to, <u>use</u> what you don't want or what you'd prefer not to have, or what you want to avoid or eliminate, to help clarify what you <u>do</u> want. Keep in mind however, the goal is to <u>determine</u> and FOCUS on what you DO want.

Renew Your Commitment To Abundance Mindset Each Moment

Know precisely what you don't want, and won't tolerate. It will help you GET SPECIFIC AND CLEAR about what you want. You want to BE PRECISE when it comes to what your DCP is. For example, when you go to a buffet, there are items you <u>want</u> and those you don't. There are those items you don't know whether you want or not. So you taste them.

If you don't like it, and don't want it, you toss it away. You don't select it again. You end up selecting and eating <u>only</u> what you do want. Similarly, with your DCP you can determine precisely what you do want by <u>knowing</u> what you don't. Perhaps, another example will help CLARIFY.

Obstacles Do Not Block The Path They Are The Path – Enjoy All

You think, "I don't want to be poor anymore." That thought alone, doesn't tell you <u>enough</u> <u>about</u> what you <u>do</u> want, but <u>now</u> you can further clarify. "I want to have enough money to live the life of my design. I want all my bills paid off and money left over at the end of the month." Are you getting this, yet? It is important YOU UNDERSTAND this.

"I want X amount of dollars in my bank account." Getting clear about what you don't want in your life helps you to identify, clarify and be specific about what you do want in your life. You must <u>get</u> this especially, as it pertains to your DCP.

People have problems in life because they create and attract what they don't want by <u>repeatedly</u> <u>focusing</u> on what they don't want. They focus on problems, debt, lack, scarcity, and more. Focus on what you do want <u>in</u> <u>order</u> <u>to</u> create what you want. <u>Use</u> what you don't want to help answer that question. Remember? Get it? It's a tool to use.

Encourage Believe And Love Yourself – Never Lose Faith In You

What do you want in a job? "I don't know." Okay, well what don't you want or what won't you do? "Okay, well I don't want to work 12 or 15 hours a day. I won't do hard or manual labor. I hate snobby coworkers. I don't want to be in a stuffy office. I hate to be bored doing the same thing again and again!"

So what would you ask this person, <u>or</u> yourself, to find the right job? Perhaps, you'd ask, "What would you like if you don't want that?" The answer might be this. "I'd like to work 8 hours in an open office, with plenty of space, where I can look out windows. I want it to challenge me and be able to utilize my creativity. I'd like new challenges often. I like computer work. I'd want to be surrounded by interesting, nice people who are going somewhere in life."

By looking at what we want and don't want we can HONE IN ON THE IDEAL target job, or goal. Do you understand how we <u>use</u> <u>these</u> <u>questions</u> to get clear about what we want and are seeking? Now you, or your friend, has a better chance of finding that kind of job. It can be aimed for.

Energy Flows Where Your Attention Goes – Focus And Flow

There is much more to clarify, but hopefully, this helps you begin to <u>understand</u> this process and get you to be specific about your DCP.

CREATE A BETTER LIFE for yourself. Stop focusing on what you don't want. WITHDRAW YOUR ATTENTION FROM PROBLEMS and what isn't working or what you don't have.

Recognize <u>when</u> you are focused on the negative, or what you don't want. <u>Then</u> shift your focus from that, to what it is you do want. PUT YOUR ATTENTION ON CREATING THE LIFE YOU WANT TO LIVE. <u>Only</u> use the question, "What is it you don't want?" to determine what it is you do want.

Fill Mind With Powerful Positivity – And You'll Change

Keep in mind you create and get what you focus on!

Therefore, you must STOP THINKING NEGATIVELY. Stop entertaining and, thereby, perpetuating problems! When you think about what's wrong, you keep it current! Stop that! Stop wasting time being distracted. Stop looking at your phone. Stop complaining about the traffic. Stop watching TV for five or six hours a day. Stop wasting your time! <u>Start</u> putting the bulk of your energy <u>into</u> your positive development.

Hill also said, in order to think and grow rich you have to make your definite chief purpose a burning desire. You must make it a white-hot obsession. It must be what you spend <u>most</u> of your time thinking about and working to make happen. We become what we think about <u>most</u> <u>frequently</u> and consistently! Get it? What we think about most often is what we then experience. We create or attract it. See this?

Direct Your Mind Where You Want To Travel – It Will Take You

The balance of your thinking and time spent must shift. Be mostly positive, not negative. Spend <u>most</u> of your time in pursuit of what you want, thinking, speaking and feeling positively as you do. That is what it means to FOCUS ON WHAT YOU WANT. Spend your time imagining the good. NOT the bad. Get it?

Concentrate on making your wants and dreams and Definite Chief Purpose happen. Dwell on these. First, you must know what you want. You must focus on what you want. You must know specifically what you want to do for your life's work. Second you must KNOW why.

Why you want it, is the motivator. It is YOUR BIG REASON you want it. That is 'why' you will, or won't, persist in making it happen, if the going gets tough. If you have wimpy reasons, don't expect to STAY TRUE TO YOUR GOAL. On the other hand if you have POWERFUL, POSITIVE REASONS and benefits, you BECOME UNSTOPPABLE. You will keep your commitment and follow through.

Whether You Think 'I Want It' Or 'No I Don't' – You Attract It

The reason you will continue is because your 'why' is the motivator. To determine the motivation, ask yourself this. "What will having what I want allow me to be, do or have? Will it result in more freedom, love, luxury, comfort, health, fun and well-being? What will be the benefits of living this life purpose? What will I be able to do as a result of accomplishing this?" Get it? What will it give you?

Stop, take a moment, and imagine you have already accomplished your DCP. This assumes you have specified it and really want it. Make a list of all the good reasons, the benefits, the emotions and positive feelings of having it right now. Imagine it yours. IMAGINE, YOU ALREADY HAVE WHAT YOU DESIRE! You have the benefits, right now. You have freedom, or love or health or fun or whatever the benefits are for you. Get it?

FEEL ALL THE GREAT FEELINGS, you'd feel, if you had it right this moment. How good does this feel? Feel it fully! Imagine this as vividly as you can.

Direct Your Mind – Ask Questions To Clarify Your Wants

If it feels wonderful and you want it even more, that is great! That is putting you right on track. That is <u>precisely</u> what you want. You want it to FEEL GOOD AND BE ENTHUSED as you think about it. Passionate is wonderful. Make this your <u>daily</u> DCP exercise.

Exercise: Imagine you have already accomplished your DCP. Be certain you have written it out already. Make sure it is specified. Make sure this is what you really want. Keep your DCP statement as brief as possible. List all the <u>good reasons</u>, the <u>benefits</u>, the emotions and <u>positive feelings</u> of having it right <u>now</u>. Once that is finished. Stop. Take a breath and begin to imagine it as yours. Imagine, you <u>already</u> have your DCP! You are right now <u>living</u> it! Feel all the great feelings! Feel it fully! <u>Savor</u> these feelings. Spend a few minutes imagining and feeling this <u>each day</u> and during the day.

A <u>good</u> practice is to write your DCP out on a pocket-sized card you can get laminated. Carry it with you and do this repeatedly, often, whenever you can throughout each day.

Happy People Choose To Be Happy

Make a laminated pocket card for any goal you have. Write out your DCP or goal. Get the card laminated. It is best to work on one goal at a time. Once your DCP is specified, if the other goals <u>are</u> <u>steps</u> toward making that happen, you could do those too, at the same time. Still, it's <u>best</u> to focus on step one, when you manifest that one, <u>then</u> move on to step two. I'll share more on this coming up.

If it feels, blah, then, perhaps what you want doesn't excite you. Your goals <u>should</u> excite you. You should feel eager, and excited and good when you think about your DCP <u>or</u> choose something else. You won't pursue it, if it is ho-hum.

Another possibility is, you're not feeling how great it feels to have it. It's only mental. You really want to <u>get a sense</u> of what it would be like to have it, right now. Feeling the feelings of having it is the most important thing you can do.

We're Living And Growing Or Withering And Dying – Choose

You want to feel the feelings and emotions you'd be feeling. You want to do this at the start and finish of each day. Visit these images and feelings and affirmations as often as possible throughout the day.

Feeling, visualizing and affirming confidently, strongly, enthusiastically and passionately consistently, repeatedly for long enough is what makes it a burning desire. It should be your burning desire, your white hot obsession.

If you feel this is important, SPEND TIME ENJOYING THESE MARVELOUS FEELINGS. Feel them frequently. Make it a point to do so often. Become deliriously obsessed.

Happy People Know It Comes From Within You – Not Without

For example, if you won a 100-million-dollar lottery right now, how would you be feeling? Imagine this! Stop, really stop, and imagine this as fully as you are able to. See, hear, feel, taste and smell. Make it vivid as possible. What would you be saying and doing?

I bet you'd be celebrating, feeling great and thinking of all the ways you'd use the money. You might be jumping up and down like they do on game shows. I bet you'd feel different because you now know your money worries are over. You are certain! You have more than enough. Right?

Feel how incredible it would be to come into 100 million dollars suddenly. Get it? Do this with your DCP and your goals. Make certain YOU FEEL AWESOME! The feelings are what helps you create them in reality!

You Become What You Think About

Imagine that you already have your big dream. It should completely WOW you. When you think about your big dream it should make you drool a little bit. It should <u>pull</u> you towards it as a powerful electromagnet would pull metal. Get excited. Be excited. <u>Feel it fully</u>.

<u>Remember</u>, in your brain it is always the present. The brain doesn't know the difference between now and then. You consciously know the difference, but your subconscious brain doesn't. Today and tomorrow are the same for it.

So don't put it off into the future. IMAGINE YOURSELF ALREADY HAVING THE GOOD YOU DESIRE. See it clearly, in detail and FEEL ALL THE WONDERFUL FEELINGS. This is what you focus on. <u>Focus on the end result</u>. The goal achieved! This is what you imagine.

<u>See</u> it through your eyes. What is your point of view? What do you see? Imagine sitting in your dream car looking through the windshield, your hands on the wheel. Imagine what it feels like to drive the dream car. Feel the seats, smell the interior, feel the grip, hear the engine and your positive self-talk. How do you sound? What do you say to yourself?

You Think 'Yes I Want It' Or 'No I Don't' You Still Create It

<u>Hear</u> what others say as they congratulate you on fulfilling your desire. Make it vivid in all of your senses. Enjoy the sights, sounds, feelings, taste and touch. Make it real. <u>Feel</u> AS IF you already have it. Drive around feeling like you are driving your dream car. Yes! That's it!

Focus on what you want. Feel <u>certain</u> YOU CAN MAKE IT HAPPEN.

BELIEVE YOU CAN! You can have this! You must believe YOU ARE WORTHY. You deserve this. You must believe you can get this. Believe YOU CAN go out and get it legally. BELIEVE YOU WILL! You will make it happen! You will do it. Believe it.

Change Your Thinking And Change Your Life

Certainty is a feeling. You may not know, yet, how you are going to make it happen, but you can feel certain that you CAN make it happen. Do you believe this? Do you believe in yourself and your ability to do whatever positive, legal things are necessary to get it? If not, you have more belief work to do.

Examine all your beliefs around this and if they are limiting, change them. Change your feeling state, too. Change your physiology. Sit, move and walk, as if you are someone who does believe this. Move and speak powerfully, and confidently. Hold your chin up, put your chest out and walk with purpose and passion. Get it? Use your energy to create the energy you want more of. Change your limiting thoughts into positive thoughts.

If you have to inch your way, do so. It's okay to be 'learning', or 'discovering' or in the process,' of getting what you want. Remember, this from affirmation practice?

Good Habits Get You What You Want To Be, Do And Have

Just make sure you shift from what stops you, or feels less than glorious, to glorious, so you move ahead. Make certain you are certain. You want what you say you do. If you still find you can't believe you will get it, and feel good about it, while you do, then chunk it down. Break it into manageable steps. Think of a smaller, yet desirable goal that would be the first step in going after your larger goal.

Then focus on that smaller step and be certain you will do that. Once you have accomplished that step, move onward to the next step. You will get there sooner this way, than any other way. Trust me. Do it.

Feel great about you're your goal or DCP. Feel it as an obsession and be certain YOU CAN MAKE IT HAPPEN. These are important steps in the sequence of creating what you want.

Love Life And You Will Get Everything You Want

Some people worry they don't know what to do. That's okay. You don't and you can't, yet. I will tell you why in a moment. You simply need to imagine it as already yours, BE INTENSELY PASSIONATE about it and feel certain you can have it. It is the feelings that drive everything. Think, "This IS mine!"

So feel certain YOU WILL bring it about even if you don't know what to do at this moment. Realize you can and learn as you go. Stay with the good feelings. TRUST YOURSELF and believe in yourself. The how will take care of itself, in time. You will learn if you STAY OPEN AND POSITIVE. If you believe in yourself, you will learn to trust yourself.

Consider this. The Wright Brothers were the first to manufacture a machine that flew. No one had ever flown in an airplane before so no one knew how to do it. They kept attempting, and making adjustments, until they got it correct. Only after they flew, did they know how to fly. Until they flew, they were experimenting.

Stop Being Critical – Learn How To Let Go And Accept

Thomas Edison tried 10,000 different times to make a working electric light. 10,000 times! He persisted because he believed he could do it. He was certain that if he kept trying he'd get it right. ONLY after he made a working one did he know how to make an electric light. Until then, for 9,999 times, he was using trial and error.

Neither of these inventive examples would have accomplished their dreams if they didn't know what they wanted. If they weren't obsessed they'd have given up. If they didn't believe they could and would succeed they would not have pursued it.

They persisted. They did not get distracted. They stayed focused. They made it happen because they were certain they would! If you do the same things, you can get similar results in your life.

The Goal Is To Feel Good Most Of The Time

Believe it. Stay with the good feelings. Where people screw it up BIG TIME is they begin to wonder how they will ever make it happen. They get concerned with whether they can afford it, do it, get it and be it. They begin to worry they might not have what it takes. Stop that! Put an end to doubt, worry and fear.

This doubt, worry, anxiety, and fear will prevent you from making it happen if you succumb to it. So, stay focused on the good feelings of having it. Feel it strongly. Enjoy and delight in it. Savor these.

The possibility exists, that if, when you think about it, you don't feel so good, or you're doubtful that you can make it happen, it only means your dream is too big for you to presently believe.

Add In New Enjoyable Behaviors

As already mentioned, you may need to make it a little smaller. Keep the big dream for the future and focus on something you believe and KNOW YOU CAN ACHIEVE. Focus on something else that makes you FEEL GOOD AND EXCITED about.

For example: You want to earn one million dollars this year but the most you have ever made is 50 thousand. Keep the Million Dollar goal as something to aim for, but consider making a smaller amount first. Something closer to what you have previously earned, but large enough to get you excited about obtaining it. Perhaps, 60 thousand dollars works, then, maybe 80 thousand, and then 100.

Think of it as taking a cross-country trip. You want to drive to L A from NYC. That is too far to drive in one session, so you make your goal a target city. Say Akron, OH and from there you proceed to

Chicago, IL from there Denver, CO and from Denver you go on to Los Angeles.

Anything You Can Imagine Can Be Yours

Simply break your big goal into smaller <u>manageable</u> bite size steps that you can more readily accomplish. As you pick up each goal your confidence in making larger goals increases. Build your success muscle and CONDITION YOURSELF all along the way. Each time you succeed you win. Each time you win, you feel better and better.

Whenever you find yourself thinking, "I don't know how I will ever do this" or some version of that doubt, you can think to yourself, "I don't know how or when I will make this happen, I <u>only know</u> that I will and I FEEL WONDERFUL AND GRATEFUL." You don't know what you don't know. So utilize it instead of making it an obstacle.

Feel Truly Grateful

You can <u>set</u> a deadline or target date. That can help. It should be <u>realistic</u> depending on what you want to accomplish. You can't expect to lose 40 pounds overnight or make a million dollars this year if you haven't. Actually, the latter is more probable but you might want to set a date a year, two or three years into the future.

There is an upside and downside to setting a date depending on your personality. If, you haven't yet made it happen, and the deadline gets closer and closer, you could end up doubting, worrying, getting scared and eventually giving up. You could think, "I knew it wouldn't happen". That is a possibility.

If you realize those thoughts are those limiting beliefs surfacing and you decide it is an opportunity to learn, <u>eliminate</u> them, CHANGE YOUR MINDSET, AND <u>GROW</u>, then it is a wonderful <u>opportunity</u>. Then whether or not you GET YOUR GOAL by your deadline you are <u>still</u> benefiting. You benefit <u>all</u> <u>along</u> the way, <u>whether</u> you hit your deadline or not. If you give up and quit, then it didn't serve you.

Love Yourself

The other possibility as it gets closer is you BECOME <u>EVEN</u> MORE DETERMINED than ever to make it happen. You pull out all stops. The impending deadline serves to <u>activate</u> you. You jump into action. You do <u>whatever</u> you can, positively and legitimately, to bring it about.

You get excited as it nears. So you get to work making it happen and you do by, on, or near the deadline. Even if you don't make it happen by the target date, you still learned and grew and benefited.

At first, it is good enough to just allow the 'when' to be whenever. The plus side is it gives you total freedom for whenever the right time is. On the other hand if it goes on too long without evidence, you could begin to doubt. Even if that occurs there is opportunity <u>if</u> you recognize the doubt <u>as</u> opportunity to change those limitations and blocks into assets.

<u>Realize</u> <u>every</u> moment <u>is</u> a moment you can use in your favor. Awareness <u>is</u> the key. RECOGNIZE OPPORTUNITY to change limiting beliefs into powerful positive beliefs <u>whenever</u> they arise. <u>Choose</u> to change them. No longer succumb to the limitations. Do this and <u>you will</u> skyrocket your abilities!

Every day can be exciting. Choose to be thrilled!

> *"Never ever underestimate the importance of having fun"*
> —— *Randy Pausch*

> *"Rich people play the money game to win. Poor people play the money game to not lose."*
> —— *T. Harv Eker*

"Rule your mind or it will rule you."
—— *Buddha*

CHAPTER EIGHTEEN

You Know More Than You Think You Do

How do you get your DCP or goal? How will it happen? How it happens is YOU MAKE IT HAPPEN. YOU will ultimately DO THE RIGHT THINGS, at the right time, to bring it about. YOU SHOULD NOT concern yourself with how you will do it. ONLY concern yourself with <u>what</u> you want, the <u>feelings</u> and <u>why</u> you want it. As you do you will <u>learn</u> to TRUST YOUR SELF.

Think, "I don't know how I am going to make this (car, or these millions, or whatever,) mine but I KNOW I WILL make this, or something better, mine. I FEEL GREAT! I'M THANKFUL."

"Right now, I don't know how I am going to make X mine (or get X), but I will, and I feel glad!" (or fantastic or great or thankful). Express your gratitude. Realize it's not 'if' you make it happen, but <u>when</u> you make it happen! Remember, knowing how now is not important. It will come to you!

As Above So Below As Within So Without

Keep in mind you don't know what you don't know. You can't. So don't worry about it. Imagine walking on a path. You go as far as you can see. Once you get there, you can see farther. Get it? You can't see around a bend in the road but once you are there you can see around the curve.

The plan to get the car or the money will unfold as you move forward. STOP WORRYING and BELIEVE IT IS POSSIBLE. Enjoy it. <u>If</u> you believe it and feel good about it, <u>you</u> can make it yours.

You simply don't know the when, yet. That is fine. Just know it is coming. Just know you are moving in the right direction. Just know you are and you will make it happen. When is not a concern, either. Get it?

Whether You Think 'I'm Rich' Or 'I Am Poor' – You Attract It

For most people their brains go haywire on this. That is because you have been conditioned from early on to work on 'the how'. Your parents, teachers, friends, everyone, most all of us, were brought up concerned with how we can make something possible.

We listened to our parents worry over bills and money and how to make ends meet. How to afford a new home? How to get an A in a class at school? How to throw a baseball better? How to be a better skateboarder or computer geek? How to get a better paying job? They and we worried over timetables, end of month, beginning of month, terms and semester deadlines. STOP! It will happen when it happens.

Those who get to the top in business, sports or any endeavor, do so because of their desire and passion. They want it. It becomes their obsession. They know why they want it. They LIVE IT, AND BREATHE IT! They keep doing. As a result, they improve. They advance! They know they <u>will</u> get it. They know they will make it happen. It is not even a question. They are certain if they want it, it will be theirs!

Whether You Think 'I Am Healthy' Or 'I Am Sick' – You Create It

It first, begins inside with mindset. They know they WILL have this. They are certain! They pour everything into making it happen. They find mentors. They observe others who successfully do what they want to. They do not let anything stop them. They keep at it. They believe! They maintain their powerful, positive mindset and enthusiasm. They stay on it! They never give up. They persist until they succeed.

Many of those born to wealth and privilege rarely concern them-selves with whether or not they will be it or have it. They <u>know</u> they will. They know <u>they</u> can afford it, so price is not an issue. Their mindset is, they are entitled to it. They deserve it, and will have it. True, they may have been brought up thinking this, but you, and I, and the rest of us can cultivate it.

This can be a great mindset to adopt. "I always get what I want. I make it happen. Even if I don't know how, I will figure it out, and IT WILL ALL COME TOGETHER WELL IN THE END. THINGS ALWAYS WORK OUT FOR THE BEST. I always land on my feet."

You, too, <u>are</u> entitled to everything good. <u>You</u> deserve it as a person born on this planet. Pompous entitlement isn't good for anyone, but understanding that <u>you</u> have as much right as anyone else, is important. If it is possible for one person, it is possible for you. Keep this in mind. KNOW THIS IN YOUR HEART.

Whether You Think 'I Am Smart' Or 'I Am Stupid' – You Are It

Mindset <u>rules</u> everything. It determines how you feel and <u>how far</u> you will go. <u>If</u> you <u>never</u> concern yourself with <u>not</u> having it, imagine how much easier it is to actually have it. <u>Read that again out loud</u> and think about the mindset that thinks that way. How incredibly powerful that is! You bring it about because you are convinced you will. You don't even consider the alternative to having it.

Not having it <u>isn't</u> an option. You act accordingly. YOU ARE CERTAIN YOU CAN DO IT. Your mindset should be positive, powerful and unstoppable. You should focus <u>solely</u> on what you want and not get distracted by anything else. Ultimately, you will get your DCP! It will come in the right time. So, STAY WITH IT. Keep the faith and keep working it. It will happen!

When you <u>repeat</u> the correct actions, <u>consistently</u>, for a long enough period of time, you <u>DEVELOP</u> A NEW HABIT. Use this process to get results. Along the journey to your destination <u>you will learn</u> what to do and what not to do. You will experiment as the Wright Brothers, Thomas Edison, Steve Jobs and others have. You will make the way.

Defeat Is Only Temporary Unless You Quit

You will DISCOVER THE POWER OF YOUR INTUITION. Listen to yourself. Pay attention to your gut feelings. Take advantage of hunches and flashes of inspiration. Act on them. Listen to your inner wisdom. As you move forward, trusting yourself, respecting yourself, not insulting or blaming yourself, you develop a harmonious relationship with your own subconscious.

Remember, YOUR SUBCONSCIOUS MIND SERVES YOU. It isn't the problem. Your conditioning is. Your conscious mind wanting something different than your subconscious mind creates the conflict. Stop rebuffing yourself. Stop blaming yourself. Stop accusing yourself for not being enough. Forgive yourself for screw-ups. Stop thinking you self-sabotage! Begin learning to love and appreciate yourself.

Then you'll begin doing the right things at the right time. You begin seeing the opportunities presented to you. You feel good and start taking inspired actions. Since you aren't insulting yourself you free up that energy to work for you. Your brain finds positive matches because you are thinking positively. You don't know what you don't know, but your subconscious mind knows more than you do. It works for you!

It Is Better To Try And Fail Than To Never Try

When you LOVE AND APPRECIATE yourself, when you are grateful for yourself and all your experiences, EVERYTHING IS A BLESSING. You begin to open the flow of intuition and positive subconscious actions and behaviors. You reveal to yourself what to do and where to go. It flows. Get it?

In the meantime when is the right time? When you get it! Stop putting your focus on anything that doesn't support or contribute to you making it happen. Get very clear about this. Remember, how and when is not important. Don't allow yourself to be distracted. In its own time, it will happen. Trust and trust yourself.

I know, for some, there might be a little difficulty embracing these concepts fully. In time you will, so relax and KNOW YOU ARE TRANSFORMING YOURSELF, even by simply exposing yourself to these concepts. Remember this, a seed planted, is harvested in time, when it is ready.

You Cannot Escape The Results Of Your Thoughts

Not before. Once planted, you must TRUST it is growing, without digging it up. That would kill it. The same applies here. Once you begin to manifest what you want, it is manifesting. Stick with it. Stay true to the process. Don't allow yourself to succumb to what doesn't help you.

We become what we think about. We get what we focus on. Stop thinking about anything that doesn't support you in making, and attracting, what you want. Stay true to the process. Drop the rest. DROP DOUBTS, WORRY, AND DISTRACTION. Don't get caught up or you'll delay it.

Focus on feeling good. FOCUS ON ENJOYING YOUR LIFE, right now. Focus on being grateful that you already have your DCP. Feel it. Be grateful for everything you do have, right now, too. Appreciate the challenges and blessings. All of it is worth learning from and enjoying. APPRECIATE AND CELEBRATE yourself. Love who and what you are.

You Are Today Where Your Thoughts Brought You

Energy flows where your attention goes. You direct it. How you spend your time is important! Spend it feeling blessed. Feel these feelings, enthusiastically. The more you feel better, more of the time, with your purpose in mind, the swifter you are able to bring it about! So relax, enjoy, and celebrate everything!

Prepare for a blessed day. Can you DISCOVER ALL THE GOOD TODAY? If your day today is almost over do it tomorrow. Now, be thankful for the day you have had.

As an ethical, moral person, you probably think, "hey, I don't want more than my fair share." But that reveals belief that wealth is limited. If you believe wealth is unlimited, there's no such thing as a share of it. Everybody's share is unlimited. There's nothing to have a share of. There's only unlimited. Your fair share is all you can possibly attract. As is anybody and everybody else's."
—— Russell Brunson

CHAPTER NINETEEN

What You Are Not Aware Of Holds You Hostage

Whatever is outside of your awareness <u>runs</u> the show. It is what is going on that you don't pay attention to that determines whether you get what you want or not. So much of our thinking is automatic and below the threshold of consciousness. It governs everything. It is subconscious.

Consider this. Most of an iceberg is hidden below the water's surface. It's massive and unseen. The tip of the iceberg is tiny by comparison. We can compare it to our conscious mind. It is what we are aware of moment to moment. The subconscious mind is everything else. We can't see and don't know what is underwater.

What is beneath the surface runs the show. Our subconscious contains the beliefs that serve us, and the ones that don't. It contains our blocks, limitations, fears, worries and habits. It is the warehouse for all of our automatic, previous conditioning. Remember, the Titanic?

You Will Be Tomorrow Where Your Thoughts Take You

It was done in by what was beneath the surface. It is the same for us. What we aren't aware of <u>runs</u> the show. In order to change we need to <u>become</u> <u>aware</u> of the habits and patterns that don't serve us. Awareness is the first key. It is like a flashlight in a dark room. It highlights things so we can notice what is there.

Once you BECOME AWARE that things aren't working as you hope they would; when YOU DISCOVER YOURSELF thinking, feeling and behaving in less than productive and positive ways; when you react out of anger, fear, worry or sadness instead of responding, it <u>is</u> a golden and opportune time.

Life on Your Terms

When you <u>notice</u> it and want to change it is <u>when</u> you can BEGIN TO MAKE THE CHANGES that count. So pretty much, it runs like this. We don't know, what we don't know. We are running on automatic. Something happens and we don't like it. We don't like what we are doing. So we DECIDE TO CHANGE.

You Cannot Escape The Results Of Your Thoughts

When you begin to TAKE CONTROL OF YOUR THINKING, you work with what you are aware of. You change the <u>obvious</u> negative thoughts you encounter into positive. You <u>recite</u> affirmations. You do this a few times a day, consistently, and over time things begin to shift.

You start experiencing success. You become aware of your thinking and your feeling. You begin to notice whether you FEEL GOOD MOST OF THE TIME or not. Life changes. The process takes a while, just as it takes a while for a plant to grow from seed to bear fruit. Still, it is good!

The subconscious works doing what it learned to do from birth onward. It is a storehouse of automatic habits, beliefs, memories and experiences from which we navigate the world. When we DECIDE TO CHANGE, we make a conscious decision to change the subconscious process.

We Are Fortunate To Become Aware Of The Content Of Our Mind

Back in the 80's or 90's Professor Peter Kuzmich Anokhin of Moscow University said that the brain is composed of ten billion neurons. He stated that each neuron can make nearly infinite connections (one with twenty-eight zeros after it). "If a single neuron has this quality of potential, we can hardly imagine what the whole brain can do..."

Our subconscious treasure chest processes trillions of bits of data each second. It runs the show. It does what it learned to do to keep

195

us the same and alive. It is our friend. The conscious mind has been said to be able to handle seven plus, or minus, two bits of data. That means we can attend to between five and nine things about every moment.

Phone numbers are ten digits, seven plus three including area code. License plates were six, now seven bits in length. We can EASILY REMEMBER these. The conscious mind doesn't nearly have the processing power of the subconscious. When there is a conflict, usually it is our conscious mind wanting something different while our subconscious mind delivers what it always, reliably has. It does what it does. Get it?

When The Going Gets Tough The Tough Get Going

Be thankful. STOP RESENTING it for doing its job well! The power of the conscious mind is in directing the subconscious. We decide consciously what we want to go after. Here is the caveat. If we don't inform and teach and train and send powerful positive, feeling messages to the subconscious it will continue to do what it always has. It does what it does. That's what it is great at.

Those who don't know any better call this self-sabotage. Those who know better like you, and like me, train it to work with us. Stop calling it a bad thing. BEFRIEND YOUR SUBCONSCIOUS. Align with it. Get it going powerfully after what it is you do want. Get this and you will have learned something of great importance. Your subconscious is also a treasure chest of resources, talents and positive abilities.

This is precisely why you want to DEVELOP A LOVING, APPRE-CIATIVE, RESPECTFUL RELATIONSHIP WITH ALL OF YOUR SELF. Accept and allow you to be who you are. End the criticizing and blaming and start encouraging and nurturing your-self. When you do, you align with the incredible power of your subconscious processes and you can make amazing things happen.

You Are Building New Neural Pathways And New Habit

I liken conscious decisions to the rudder steering a large ship. The subconscious is a huge, vast, storehouse of power and resources. It contains the energy and mechanisms to move and turn the ship in the direction the conscious mind determines.

We direct the subconscious! We train and condition it through correct repetition of strong emotions, affirmations and visualization. We DO THIS REPEATEDLY to get it to learn what we want it to do now. Through proper repetition we condition the mind and CREATE NEW SUBCONSCIOUS HABITS.

We consciously direct the subconscious mind. It carries out the processes. Get it? We decide. It does the work. It is like riding a horse. We direct it where to go and the horse does the work to get us there.

You Are A Powerful Creator

During the process of evolving ourselves into deliberate positive manifestors, there are still old habits of thought that continue. Many are petty thoughts, sometimes, about nothing in particular. We don't think about them, we just think them. We barely ever notice them unless the signal value becomes loud enough.

Thoughts dictate our experience. They govern our day. Because we don't notice them, we don't change them. They are chatter. They are mostly less than glorious, maybe neutral, but make up negative commentary or narration about our daily experiences.

I'll give you an example I hope illuminates. I am in the lap pool doing laps and enjoying. A woman comes in, could have been anyone actually, man or woman. She is new. She stops me to ask how she gets into my lane. I tell her duck under the buoys. This bothers her.

Become Aware Of What You Are Thinking

She doesn't want to get her hair wet. I noticed when she entered the pool she hadn't showered. This bothered me. I didn't say anything. Anyway, she does her thing. Soon, she grabs some floats off the poolside, which a handicapped man had been using, and takes them for herself.

He points this out to me. I get out of the pool, go get him some more dumbbell floats and give them to him. She appears oblivious. Too concerned with not getting her hair wet, apparently. I think. He thanks me and begins his exercise. I return to my lane and she joins me.

She gets into my lane in front of me. She moves slowly in front of me. She walks slower than I had been moving. She starts a conversation with another woman in the center lane and they walk slowly. In my lane she moves down the middle, her arms out to both sides. I am becoming annoyed. It goes on.

Once Aware – We Can Move From Chaos And Misery To Bliss

I begin thinking, "Who does she think she is? Why does she come here and get into my lane?" I think, "If you are going to be here get wet, go all in. How about being aware of others. There were plenty of floats on the rack why didn't you pick one of those?" Soon, I notice.

I noticed I began feeling less than glorious. My attention had shifted from how much I enjoyed the water, the day, my time in the pool to "How dare this interloper come in here and have no regard for anyone." "Who does she think she is?" Okay, I didn't actually think the word interloper. It was a stronger word I thought.

Then, I realized I was spiraling downward. I wasn't angry. I was annoyed. I felt less than glorious. I realized my thoughts were running on about something that wasn't important. I was spending time thinking and reacting to what I didn't want. I was caught up. I was running habitual, subconscious patterns and commentary. More of my time was thinking less than glorious thoughts, than glorious ones.

If You Want To End Negativity Become Aware Of Positive Things

It was the monkey mind running from treetop to treetop chattering at everything below. Do you understand? I wasn't in charge. It was running me. As I became aware of it I thought, "Whoa! Stop! THINK AND SPEAK ONLY TO BLESS, HEAL AND PROSPER. Stop giving this attention."

I remembered Jesus' saying; "Forgive them for they know not what they do". Clearly, this woman didn't know how I was being affected AND I could forgive! She hadn't really done anything wrong. It was just whatever she was doing bumped up against how I thought things should be. Rules. Beliefs. They are our subconscious patterns and habits.

When I became aware I was letting my mind drive me into unpleasantness, I shifted it. I realized I had spent a good number of minutes experiencing unpleasantness all between my own ears. I was looking through my eyes but my discomfort came from within.

Stay Positive In Thoughts And Feelings

The rest of the day I became aware of thoughts on things I could not change. I noticed that if someone, or something, upset me how I wanted to think those thoughts, again and again. There was a natural tendency to re-live the discomfort and to try to solve it.

Almost as if, I could play the thoughts over, and over enough, I might be able to FEEL BETTER by finding the right thing to think, say or do. I was mentally planning what to do if this ever happened to occur again. Actually, I was just getting caught in a negative loop that ran endlessly while making me feel worse. INSIGHT! Ding, Ding, Ding, Ding, Ding!

Let it go. The thoughts returned. I repeatedly had to put them aside and think what I wanted. I learned there's a lot of automatic BS that goes on, about trying to control situations. I discovered I had lots of rules on how people should conform and behave.

Awareness Allows Us To Escape The Trap Of Our Daily Lives

These are all junk thoughts! These are junk thoughts about everyday things. They are just petty everyday nuisances that chew up time and energy. Most of the time these thoughts operate outside awareness but they use up critical energy. As I became more aware of these, I could let them go and shift to the positive.

Only as I became more aware of the less than glorious chatter, and let it go, did I become free. Once aware, I could drop them. As long as it ran on below threshold, it dictated my experience. This is how many of us spend our days. These kinds of thoughts lead to stress and discomfort. We are the thinker, not the thoughts!

Remember, we become what we think about most of the time. I would never have been able to notice them, nor alter them, and change my experience from less than glorious to feeling good, without all my previous work. What made the difference for me now, was all my previous work on taking charge of my thoughts, to begin with.

There Is So Much To Be Thankful For That We Miss

We first begin to change the things with the highest signal value. Those thoughts and feelings we are most aware of. The ones that are the loudest are the ones we first notice. Gradually, because of these efforts, we can recognize more of the subtle ones that hold us back or keep us stuck. Once aware of anything that holds us back, or spirals us downward, we can KEEP MAKING CHANGES that move us forward.

We CAN TRANSFORM ourselves by the renewing of our minds. It requires dedication and awareness. At an earlier point in my life

I'd have been disappointed to discover the monkey mind chatter. I'd have thought, "I should be beyond that". Instead, I now, could celebrate.

Anytime, we can find that which frees us up to ENJOY MORE of the wonderful opportunities living provides for us, we can DELIGHT. The more we FEEL WONDERFUL, and think wonderfully, the more we create a wonderful life. It all works together. So BECOME AWARE. Delight in all.

Change Comes From Doing The Same Things Differently

Become free. Take control of your thoughts and feelings. It is worth it! Nothing feels as marvelous and helps us enjoy the life we live, as when we GET FREE FROM PAST, old, borrowed, chronic, habitual conditioning. There is no reason to live that way, when we can live renewed.

Find gratefulness in everything. Enjoy and delight. Don't let other people or circumstances rain on your parade. Just as I discovered, it wasn't the woman who was bothering me. It was my own thought process. My thinking was causing my hell, not her.

I used her as an excuse. She was someone to blame. I had shifted the focus from what I was doing to what she was doing. That is how we live much of the time. It is what causes our suffering. Stop! Notice. BECOME AWARE. CHANGE YOUR THOUGHTS. BE POSITIVE!

Be Transformed By The Renewing Of Your Mind

STOP BLAMING outside yourself. It really isn't about others, events or circumstances. We just typically think it is because that is what we were raised to think. The discomfort doesn't come from outside us. It comes from within each of us. It's due to old thought habits. TAKE RESPONSIBILITY. Take the right actions to be free of negative thoughts.

STOP BLAMING YOURSELF! Stop the blame, the excuses and whining. Become aware, let go and get <u>free</u> from old thought habits. Through awareness begin to <u>transform</u> your thinking, your feelings, and your actions to get positive new results.

The big issue is that, most people spend most of their time, thinking on distractions, petty issues, major issues, Facebook, the news and all sorts of less than productive thoughts. They feel ho-hum, okay or less than glorious. Napoleon Hill points out that if you want to accomplish your Definite Chief Purpose you <u>need</u> <u>to</u> <u>make</u> <u>it</u> an obsession. Think about it day and night.

Start Believing In Yourself

95-99% of our thinking is unconscious habit. That means outside our awareness. These 60,000 thoughts we think daily are basically the same. In order for us to change, we need to <u>change</u> the bulk of these thoughts into powerful, productive, positive thoughts that promote wildly wonderful, positive emotions and feelings. Then we <u>will</u> want to take inspired actions to bring about our Definite Chief Purpose.

Do you see how these principles I am sharing interrelate with one another?

Think of it this way. You have a two giant energy balloons floating in space above you. One is positive and one negative. Whichever is larger dictates what you feel and what you get. Use this image to promote change. Feed the positive one positive energy and grow it larger and larger. As you do this you will notice yourself changing. That which you think of most, and most often, determines what you get. The dog you feed grows stronger. Get it?

Exercise: 10 minutes. Focus on your breath. Notice the in breath and out breath. Calm yourself down. <u>Pay</u> <u>attention</u> only to your breath. Feel the rise and fall. Notice it. Become <u>aware</u> of when thoughts creep in. It's okay. Don't judge. Just <u>notice</u> when you find yourself thinking instead of watching or paying attention to your breathing. Simply notice and return your attention, each time, back to your breath.

Go First – Be It – Then Do It To Have It

This exercise is about focus, concentration, awareness and not judging. Focus. Concentrate on your in and out breath. Become aware when you are distracted by thought. Don't judge the thoughts. Just be aware of them. Let go and return to focusing and concentrating on your breathing.

Do not judge yourself, either, when you notice your attention has lapsed, gently return to your breath. If anything, be glad you noticed the lapse so you could steer it back to your breathing. Pat yourself on the back for becoming more aware.

Positive acknowledgement helps ensure you do it again. When you are critical of yourself it doesn't help anything. It only makes you feel bad. The goal is to FEEL GOOD. When you encourage you CREATE MORE OF THE BEHAVIOR YOU WANT.

Your judgment or your praise are just more thoughts. However, one supports you better than the other. Encourage yourself to be aware of your breathing. Notice it. Notice when you are thinking other thoughts and GENTLY steer them back to your breath.

There are many benefits to this exercise. One important one is to increase your moments of awareness. It is through awareness we have the opportunity to change.

Feeling Good Is Feeling Good Is Feeling Good

Once you get good at concentrating on your breath and returning your attention to it, if you should drift, you might add this additional component: Notice whether the thoughts are supportive or non-supportive. Are they positive or negative? What are you thinking? Simply notice and return your attention, each time, back to your breath. Be an observer. Be a witness. Just watch. Realize and remember, you get what you think about, whether you want it or not.

In order to change become aware. Let go of the issues and become grateful you recognized an opportunity to transform. It is in these moments we can make giant leaps ahead. So it is important to learn to celebrate everything!

How many different ways can you find to feel marvelous today?

"What you think you become. What you feel you attract. What you imagine you create."
—— Buddha

"Many people are like garbage trucks. They run around full of garbage, full of frustration, full of anger, and full of disappointment. As their garbage piles up, they look for a place to dump it. And if you let them, they'll dump it on you. So when someone wants to dump on you, don't take it personally. Just smile, wave, wish them well, and move on. Believe me. You'll be happier."
—— David J. Pollay

"God did not create you to fail!"
—— Tommy Coletta

"If you can't do anything about it then let it go. Don't be a prisoner of things you can't change."
—— Tony Gaskins

"Waking up to who you are requires letting go of who you imagine yourself to be."
—— Alan Watts

CHAPTER TWENTY

Stop Creating Trauma, Drama And Crap In Your Life

How much more can you smile today?

You try, but screw up. Things don't work out. You end up with crap. Have you felt like this? You spin your wheels trying to get out of debt or overcome difficulty. What on earth is going on? Why does it seem so hard? Would you like to know what you can do to change this?

Would you like to know what is possibly going on? From one standpoint, the answer is simple. Negative manifestation. You are creating the opposite of what you want. The results you keep getting are not the results you want to get. So why does it keep happening? What must you do differently to change it?

Napoleon Hill said, "If you can conceive it and believe it you can achieve it." That's what most people do to bring about disasters. If you are like most people it is because of what your focus is on. It is how you USE YOUR MIND. We all tend to do this! We imagine the bad things happening. Put that in your past!

Our Feelings Are The Product Of What We Think

People don't realize they are already powerful creators. We have been conditioned to believe that things just happen to us. It is true, they do. We are taught to believe we have no control over our circumstances, and to an extent, this is accurate as well. Things happen and influence us

However, if you want to change your lot in life, there are some simple things you must do. The first is to adjust your mindset and TAKE 100% RESPONSIBILITY for everything that happens to you. You must understand you create it all. Even, if that statement is not completely true, accept it as fact, and act as if it is. It is a useful re-frame. Use it to your benefit.

When you ACCEPT FULL RESPONSIBILITY for everything going on, you begin to ACCESS YOUR INNER STRENGTHS and power. Even if you don't actually create it, if you act as if it you do, if you accept responsibility for it, you begin to have a say in it. Think about it. If you are responsible for doing it, then you can change it. Then, you won't blame or excuse.

Our Results Are The Product Of What We Think

When you accept responsibility your mind begins to LOOK FOR SOLUTIONS because you are responsible. If you got yourself into it, YOU can get yourself out of it. Most people don't want to accept responsibility because of their previous, negative, chronic, conditioning. They want to blame others, circumstances, events and things for their problems, because that is what they have ALWAYS done.

By blaming they miss out on tapping into their power. It is a natural tendency to blame and excuse, to point fingers, and to find fault elsewhere. Blame and excuses don't actually help anything. It doesn't help to blame others or circumstances or oneself. Stop it!

Let go of the blame. Accept responsibility for what is. Then shift your focus from what is going on, to what you want to be going on, instead. Move your attention from the crap to the potential. FOCUS ON THE DESIRED OUTCOME, not present circumstances. Get it? Stop it, from being a problem for yourself.

The Moment You Take Full Responsibility – Everything Changes

The reason people have problems, is that most people imagine bad things happening. They run movies in their head about negative results. They imagine the axe falling. Then it does. They focus on the difficulty. They worry and fear bad things. Then they get bad things. They don't think they are creating bad things, just that bad things happen to them. It is habitual, unconscious and outside of awareness.

They succeed in helping make the bad thing happen. They create it. They support it. They allow it. Even though they don't want it, they attract it. In order to change your current reality, from not so great to better or to great, you must understand this principle.

Even if you don't think it is true, if you accept it as if it were, and act accordingly, you will begin to EXPERIENCE POSITIVE CHANGE. You may create great positive change! But, to do so you must embrace it and live from it. You must understand it and change what you are doing.

You Cannot Escape The Consequences Of Your Thoughts

Here is the principle; the universe ONLY says 'Yes.' Just like your subconscious mind. In fact, it could be both, or one in the same. Whatever you think about most you get, whether you want it or not! Get it?

You get whatever you want or whatever you don't want by what you PUT YOUR ATTENTION on most often, consistently, with intensity. If you say, "no, I don't want it," you get more of it. If you say, "yes, I want it," you get more of it. That is how it works.

It is just like gravity. It pulls but doesn't choose. It always works. It doesn't judge. Whether you want it to or not, it operates. The subconscious doesn't process negation, you may recall. Remember, don't think of a blue elephant wearing a yellow hat. Oops, too late.

You Just Have To Tap Into It

Many people are attracting exactly what they don't want for these very reasons. Creating and attracting is ALWAYS ongoing. You cannot stop or prevent it.

You get whatever you are thinking about most, unconsciously! In order to change that for the better, you must consciously change it.

If you keep doing what is getting you the negative results you will never get positive ones.

You must re-write the subconscious programming and create new thought habits. It is a matter of aiming your mind and energy at what you want. Withdraw your energy from what you don't want.

Choose - You Are Either Positive Or Negative

Focus on GOOD THINGS. Focus on what you want. This is a main tenant of this book. You have the ability and the power to AIM YOUR MIND, whether or not you ever realize you have this ability. Unrealized, you will haphazardly use it without knowing it, to get haphazard and mostly, less than glorious results. Once you realize it, you can begin to aim your mind like a laser TO GET WHAT YOU WANT to have more of. Get It? Awareness is the first step!

You get back whatever you put out. Imagine standing in front of your bathroom mirror and you smile. What do you see reflected back at you? Imagine standing there and frowning. What do you see back at you? Now make a worried, anxious face. What is reflected back?

The principle is attraction. You attract back whatever you are! If you are worried about something you end up with more to worry about. Most people are exquisite creators of crap. Crap magnets! They want it to be different, but they keep doing the same things.

You Are Already A Powerful Creator – Now Own Up To It

If you do the same things again and again, you don't get different results. If you frown into the mirror you don't get back smiles. It would be silly to expect to. To get smiles you must be smiling! If you accept this, and determine to work with this, you can make changes.

People are successful at creating crap. Get It? They are successfully creating crap. Success breeds success. The more you practice something <u>the better you become</u>. People are really good at creating poverty, lack of love, trauma drama and lots of negative experiences. This is because that is what they grew up doing. They didn't, and they still don't, know any better.

No one told them there is a <u>better</u> way. A few stumble on these principles, fewer still, <u>learn</u> them from others. Some luck into unconsciously applying the principles, even though they never were consciously exposed to them. Only when you consciously, DELIBERATELY, <u>APPLY</u> THESE PRINCIPLES, are you most likely TO MAKE THE CHANGES YOU WANT TO MAKE.

You Are Already A Powerful Attractor – Now Own Up To It

Are you tired of trauma drama? If you are getting lackluster results you can change it. If you like what you are getting, keep on doing what you are doing. Keep on getting <u>good</u> results. Something you are doing is working! Hooray! If you don't enjoy your present circumstances, and <u>you</u> want better, then there <u>are</u> things you can put into motion that help.

You can stop <u>creating</u> the life you don't want, and begin to CREATE THE LIFE YOU WANT; using the very same process you have already been using, mentioned by Napoleon Hill. Instead of conceiving or imagining dire results, IMAGINE THE <u>GOOD</u> RESULTS you want instead. See the good.

Use the very same process that you've already been using to get what you don't want in life, to begin getting what you do want. TAKE CONTROL OF YOUR MIND AND FOCUS IT POWERFULLY, AND POSITIVELY, on what it is you DO want. Maintain the <u>focus</u> on what is <u>good</u> and what is <u>positive</u>. Keep this focus! <u>Aim</u> your mind! Remember, I mean, your <u>thoughts</u> and most importantly, your feelings.

Inside All Hardship Are Lessons And Opportunity

Then believe that you're going to get that, without any doubts. BELIEVE, BE CERTAIN, YOU WILL make it happen, and you will end up bringing that about. Certainty is a positive creative force. We need to learn how to harness it. You complain, "I don't know how to believe," or "I have doubts, what to do?" Great questions. As mentioned before, here again, is how to develop belief resulting in certainty.

Napoleon Hill pointed out, "A lie repeated often enough often becomes substituted for the truth". He encouraged people to determine their DCP, write it out and read it out loud, with powerful strong emotions, at least twice a day. "A lie repeated often enough often becomes substituted for the truth". He encouraged people to determine their DCP, write it out and read it out loud, with powerful strong emotions, at least twice a day. Imagine already having accomplished it and feel all the good feelings. See what you would be seeing, hear what you would be hearing and feel all the strong positive, wonderful feelings and emotions. KEEP REPEATING THIS DAILY. Draw your attention to this as often as you can.

It Is Simple – Do It

Expect it to come to you. Don't keep asking. Once is actually enough. Still, you want to believe it. Simply keep focused on the feelings of already having it while you affirm and visualize. It is coming just like the weekend is coming. The when or how doesn't matter. It will be here. Stay with the task at hand.

Through repetition you will eventually come to BELIEVE IT and desire it even more. He pointed out that good children and adults often go 'bad' or commit crimes through exposure to criminal acts. At first they are repulsed but eventually, given more exposure, they accept and then potentially embrace criminal activity. Once they grow accustomed to it, it is not a far cry from engaging in it. They begin to accept it.

Keep this in mind: We grow tolerant of violence in movies from repeated exposure. We can LEARN to like things we don't like or approve of. Research has been demonstrated that most people can learn to like foods they have a strong aversion for by repeatedly tasting it a little bit over a period of time. Research states it takes at least about a dozen exposures to acquire a new taste in food.

Feel Your Way To Happiness And Success

Repeatedly expose your mind to positive thoughts, feelings and actions and you accept them. What you first may doubt you BEGIN TO BELIEVE. It grows stronger and stronger the more you repeat it, over time. Consider this: you can't play the piano but you want to. THE MORE YOU PRACTICE THE BETTER YOU GET. The better you get the more confident you become.

At some point you consider yourself a piano player, or one who can play the piano. You transformed yourself by continuing to PRACTICE AND REPEAT and rehearse what is important to you. It is the same with developing positive strong beliefs and feelings. It is the same with becoming a positive and consistent manifestor or deliberate creator.

Success breeds competence, more success and confidence. You get good at it. The more you practice positivity and manifesting abundantly in your life the easier it becomes. The more confident you become, the more successes you have. It works this way. You must do it to experience it. I can tell you about it all day long and that won't change your life. You must APPLY WHAT YOU LEARN to get the results you want.

Whatever You Resist Persists

Take action with this material. Use what you read in this book now and each and every day. You will be excited with the results you can get. I encourage you to continue to feed your mind. Read and reread this material. Study it. Take handwritten notes.

Rewrite your notes at a future time. Keep reading this book. Share concepts with others because you learn when sharing. Keep at it! Study and apply this and you talents will soar. Transform yourself. Become this material. Develop unconscious competence or mastery and you will have new automatic reliable skill habits. You will WOW yourself eventually.

How soon will you see results? That is up to you.

Belief in your ability to accomplish your goals and dreams comes from maintaining continual focus on your goals, while affirming them in your mind. Use positive strong emotions. FEEL HAPPY. Feel good.

Decide What Kind Of Creator And Magnet Your Are Going To Be

When you fear the consequences, crap results. THAT is a strong emotion. When you feel fear, worry, sadness, anger, you lock yourself up. When you think and imagine bad outcomes, and feel frustrated or lost, you combine your imagination with strong negative emotions. That IS how you create the mess. That is how people stay stuck in a less than glorious, current, reality.

To GET THE BEST RESULTS you need to imagine what you want, while feeling the best feelings. FEEL CONFIDENT, HAPPY, ENTHUSED, AND EXHILARATED! Get it? You actually use this same formula for creating crap. Stop that! Now, instead, aim your mind with different, positive, components.

Imagine what you want while feeling fully confident. Feel fully confident while you imagine what you want.

Stop and consider this for a moment! Have you ever known, for sure, something bad was going to happen, and it did? It's like you predicted it. Right? Some people are certain they won't have enough money at the end of the month and they worry about it.

They feel dread. At the end of the month, guess what? They don't have any money. WOW, can you see how they used their imagination to stay broke?

Will: Separates The Successful From The Unsuccessful

Frequently, it turns out as expected. These people use their minds, powerfully, to succeed at getting exactly what they <u>do not</u> want, whenever they do this. You will too <u>and</u> continue to for as long as you do the same or similar things. That is why you must stop doing those things. Stop repeating the old way!

Most people could use their minds to get better results, but frankly, they never really listened, when they were told they could. They couldn't hear it. In many cases, they were never, ever even told.

If You Aren't In Charge – Who Did You Give The Charge To

We grew up blaming outside ourselves and worrying about circumstances. We weren't told we could be the Master of our circumstances. So, we practiced creating and attracting a lot of crap. We practiced screwing it up until we got really good at it. Oh, yes, sometimes we also make some pretty good things happen, but not consistently. Mostly, we create, just an okay life with lots of trauma drama.

For too many people life is just okay, instead of incredible. Let's make it incredible, instead! I've just described the process most of us use to create crap in our lives. You're using this method and it works. It always works! It doesn't stop working. The process doesn't judge good or bad, right or wrong, or positive or negative. It just says, 'yes' to whatever is offered it.

So, what are you aimed at? What are you aimed at <u>most</u> of the time? Are your subconscious programs and thinking habits supporting you or not? If not, then change them. Aim them in a <u>positive</u> direction. Aim them at what you want. Aim them at what you can and will do to make it all happen.

You Must Ask Believing

You must, if you want to get the positive results you desire. Nothing will change unless you CHANGE YOURSELF POSITIVELY AND WHAT YOU ARE DOING.

You can't continue to do the same old things over and over and over again and expect anything to be different. That would be insane. Yet, that is what most people do. They repeat their failures and whine and blame and excuse. Then they do it all over again. Then, again! And then again after that, still wondering why nothing changes! All the while, wondering, how come they are so unlucky and don't get breaks? Get it? The repeat and rehearse failure and crap and wonder why they keep getting it. Duh?

STOP! If you have been doing this, okay. Enough already! NOW STOP! Become aware. Take a deep breath. Change it! The results you end up with depend on how you use your mind. YOU get what YOU focus on. Get it? Yes, maybe? Time to let it go. Drop it. Don't judge, just let it go. Forgive.

What You Feel Is What You Get – You Get What You Focus On

The easiest way to change it is to focus on feeling your best. Do those little and positive things that bring you MORE ENJOY-MENT throughout each day. Find ways to smile and laugh more. Remember, you get back what you put out. APPRECIATE WHAT YOU HAVE. Enjoy it!

Be truly grateful. Feel it. Let the mirror give you back wonderful feelings by feeling wonderful first. How do you Feel Wonderful, you ask? You create wonderful feelings BY what you focus on. If you worry about crap you will feel crappy and worried. You must change your thoughts. Get it? Maybe, you do.

You must change what you give your energy and attention to. Perhaps, you have to change your thoughts dozens of times in an hour but <u>that</u> <u>is</u> what you must do. If you do it, you will gain <u>control</u> of it, eventually.

Expect It – Know It – Know What You Want – Be Clear – Precise

You get back what you <u>practice</u>. Success breeds success. The more you succeed in changing your thoughts to the positive, the easier it becomes and the <u>better</u> you feel. Now, are you beginning to get it?

You won't if you just read about it and don't apply what you are learning. The proper fruit of knowledge is action. You must APPLY WHAT YOU LEARN here to get the results you want. You must be deliberate and intend to make changes, not just wish and hope they happen for you. Most people only hope and then wonder why they remain stuck. BE DIFFERENT.

Think positive, happy thoughts. <u>Train</u> yourself to do this. No one can do it for you. <u>YOU</u> HAVE TO DO IT. It requires commitment and persistence. The payoff is spectacular! Think better thoughts and you feel better. Think better thoughts and you get better results. Remember, the mirror reflects who you <u>already</u> are. You get back what you put out there. Smile into the mirror.

I must keep repeating these principles to drive them home. Notice from moment to moment your feelings. Are you feeling positive or not? Are you feeling good? If not, shift your thoughts so that you do FEEL GOOD! Thoughts precede action. It is difficult to go uphill thinking downhill thoughts. Your thoughts determine how and what you <u>feel</u>.

<u>FOCUS ON THE GOOD</u> you already have and <u>FEEL GRATE-FUL.</u> Take some time for yourself. Get a massage. Have a bath. Read something nice. Have an enjoyable meal. Exercise. Skip, sing. Explore outdoors. Help someone else feel good. Treat yourself. Treat someone else. Change your mind. Change your state of being. Hang around with positive, upbeat people. Take an inspiring, motivational seminar or workshop. Listen to inspirational audios. FEEL BETTER. These are some actions you can do to enjoy things more.

Accept Total Responsibility For Your Life

Don't wait. Those who wait – wait. Be proactive. If you want to feel better you can't wallow in the muck. You have to get yourself out of the muck. Then, leave the muck alone. Drop it. Let it go and move to where you'd rather be. FEEL GOOD!

Some people leave and miss the muck. STOP! Don't, do that! FEEL GOOD, instead. If it is to be, it is up to you. You can change it. You can do it. If you realize you, alone, are responsible for everything, you will take charge, because you don't expect anyone else to swoop in to save you. You don't expect things to magically change without you doing it. Do you? No! It is you. You do it!

You keep doing it. You live from courage and discipline and positively charged power. Positive thinking may not solve everything but it is far better than negative thinking. If you want to FEEL GREAT, you have to THINK GREAT, too! SMILE and the mirror smiles back!

Only You Will Get You Where You Want To Go

At any moment you can wonder what is in your mirror. Take a look. If it isn't what you want, MAKE IT SO it is. Create what you want. CHANGE YOURSELF so what is reflected back IS what you want. Be the change you want more of. Enjoy the best feelings you have. Then keep on smiling! CELEBRATE EVERYTHING!

What will you reflect on today?

"If you can tune into your purpose and really align with it, setting goals so that your vision is an expression of that purpose, then life flows much more easily."
— *Jack Canfield*

CHAPTER TWENTY-ONE
The Secret To Success Few Realize: Actor's Improv Training

Among other things I am an actor. I have been since I was three. I love it. As an actor there are many forms of training, scene work, theater or on camera, commercials, audition and improv. Believe me, there are many other approaches to this art and craft. I mention this one because there is an important concept I hope you will grasp.

The art of improv means spontaneous, extemporaneous, think on your feet, (comedy, as is popularized by clubs, but there is also dramatic improv) acting entertainment. So let's deal with what most people might know, the improv club. You go, have a few drinks or food and watch people respond to audience requests.

Topics, chosen out of a hat, so to speak are blended together in unique ways. Actors work together to entertain. Here's an important principle of Improv. In order for actors to advance the premise and the scene they each must SAY, "YES" to whatever is offered. Say "Yes" and you have forward progress. Say "No", and the scene stops.

Live, Love, Laugh, Celebrate And Enjoy

It requires training to get the acting talent to go for the "Yes" right out of the gate. The ball keeps rolling as long as the actors say "Yes". The word isn't spoken out loud necessarily, though it could be. It is a principle or rule that governs the performance.

The principle for good Improv is to accept and say "Yes" to what-ever is offered you. Then, add to it to keep the ball rolling. You steer it. Your partners respond likewise. Together, you keep it moving along.

In '4 Rules Of Innovation' from her book *Bossypants*, Tina Fey says, "The first rule of improvisation is to AGREE. Saying 'No' grinds invention, innovation (and improv) to a screeching halt.

Obviously in real life you're not always going to agree with what everyone says. But saying 'YES' reminds you to respect what your partner has created and to start from an open-minded place. Start with a 'YES' and see where that takes you."

Wake Up And Live

Fey says "The second rule of improv is to not only say 'YES', say 'YES, AND'. In improv, you agree and then add something of your own. If your partner starts with, 'I can't believe it's so hot in here,' and you just say 'Yeah...' the skit has stalled. But if you respond with, 'What did you expect? We're in hell!' things keep moving forward."

I'll let you read her book to find the other two rules, but I will nutshell it for you by briefly by quoting her again. "Whatever the problem be part of the solution." and "there are no mistakes, only opportunities. The next big laugh is around the corner." I love this and it fits so well with the philosophy and approaches I have been sharing in this book, my Mind Design™ workshops and my daily blog.

I was reminded of this listening to friend, Casting Director, and expert, Amy Jo Berman implore actors to get improv training. That way when things get switched up on them at an audition or when the pages of script are changed on them moments prior to going before the casting director, they are prepared. They are skilled, well trained talent, and able to say "Yes". Nothing throws them!

Be Happy Smile More

I want to thank Tina and Amy for such great insight. I want to thank all those from ancient texts to modern day authors who have said the same thing, forever, in so many inspiring ways.

What we need to do is HEAR THE MESSAGE and then ACT ON IT. This is another reason why repetition is so necessary. Too often, we miss what is really important!

As an actor in life we need to accept and affirm whatever is handed to us. Say "Yes" and add to it. Don't let it stop there. We can steer it, just don't resist it. Direct the energies in productive ways.

Manifesting And Creating Is Fun – Delight And Celebrate

See it all the way through to the conclusion. Let go of preconceived notions of how things should be and GO WITH THE FLOW. Create some flow. Allow it to become better. Attitude is everything. HAVE FUN and learn!

The more you practice these life skills the better you get at it, just as actors do practicing and rehearsing their craft. If you do it and repeat it, again and again, correctly, you get better at it. YOU DEVELOP RELIABLE, HABITUAL SKILLS. You evolve new neural pathways that serve you better.

"Start with a yes and see where that takes you". Make it a habit to affirm life, cooperate with others, move forward, and add value to all. Practice play. Smile and laugh, lots. When doing the exercises in this book take them seriously, but not too seriously. KEEP EVERYTHING LIGHT! Make it enjoyable. You will get back more of the same. Whatever you put out there. Have fun! Play a lot.

Yes I Can

Keep moving it forward in positive ways. SO when life, or someone, throws you a curveball you step in to bat. You aren't thrown by changes. Step up to the plate when life switches things up. Go for the run.

SAY "YES" AND MOVE FORWARD. Opportunity exists and the next big one is around the corner. Remember that! Set your attitude right and you can be, do and have anything. LIVE, LOVE, LAUGH and say "Yes" to life! CELEBRATE! Celebrate everything!

Enjoy each day more than the last!

"If you're wasting time having fun, you're not wasting time."
—— *Tim Ferriss*

"You will receive what you ask for no more, no less."
—— *Mark Allen*

"You are not broken. You are not a problem to be solved. Solving your "problem", whatever you perceive your problem or problems to be, is not the key to happiness."
—— *Golda Poretsky*

"When you are inspired by some great purpose, some extraordinary project, all your thoughts break their bonds: Your mind transcends limitations, your consciousness expands in every direction, and you find yourself in a new, great, and wonderful world. Dormant forces, faculties and talents become alive, and your discover yourself to be a greater person by far than you ever dreamed yourself to be."
—— *Patanjali*

CHAPTER TWENTY-TWO

Time Is Not The Enemy But Your Friend

You have changes you want to make in your career or your life. Perhaps, you are going through difficult times. You want relief. You have developed a better attitude and are moving in the right direction. Only it doesn't seem fast enough, right?

Some people, who learn about Intentional Creation, Positive Thinking, or the Law of Attraction give it a try, and if they don't get immediate success, they decide whatever they are doing isn't working and abandon it. They want improvement overnight.

Instead of hanging in there, they claim whatever they tried didn't work, or at least not for them. No one can estimate the time it will take for you, because no one else is you. I can't tell you how well, or even if, you will actually apply these principles. My assessment of you doesn't matter.

The More We Do The More We Can Do

If you decide to stick with it, then how long will it take? It takes whatever time it takes for a seed to grow and to flower. I'm sure you already understand this. Everything takes some time. Why does it take time? Because it does! Get over it already.

Another reason is, you actually wouldn't be happy with immediate manifestation because it would work both ways. You'd create instant success or instant failure depending on what you are predominantly thinking. What a rollercoaster ride that'd be. So, that is why it takes some time to manifest. BE THANKFUL!

There is a much better reason. Not because anyone ordains it the answer, but it just seems to work this way. The reason things take time is so that you can get to be better. The reason things take time is so it is attributable to your efforts and not luck or accident. That way, you take credit for your creating.

Time Shows Us What Really Matters

Things don't manifest right away to give you PRACTICE. Time allows you to DEVELOP GOOD HABITS. You can build the habit of right thinking through time. Otherwise, you would think it is luck. You don't benefit from luck. Your greatest benefit is from truly conditioning your mind.

Once you CONDITION YOUR MIND, once you learn how to CONTROL YOUR THINKING, then anything can be yours. You become more powerful, and wise through experience because things take time. You evolve and develop your attitude, abilities and talents. You improve!

The more we do, the more we can do, is one of my favorite sayings. Things take time so you can grow and develop your skills to become more of whoever and whatever you want to be. You learn the nuance of great power and deliberate attention and control.

Stretch Beyond Your Limits Into New Ways Of Being

Rob was a student of mine who came to one of my Mind Design™ workshops with the secret dream to be a public speaker. To say he was unassuming, and the least likely candidate for being a public speaker, is an understatement. He lacked energy and enthusiasm. His body, movement and speech were tight and constrained. He looked stressed most of the time. He harbored this secret and did not reveal it to me, or anyone.

I invited him to participate in a demonstration in the front of the class. He was both reluctant and willing. Coincidentally, my demonstration was in becoming more expressive, easy-going, and relaxed. I wanted to help him release the blocks that were preventing him from feeling more joy and comfort.

In front of the room I asked him to do what I did. Standing face to face I placed my palms together at heart level, in a prayer or 'Namaste' position and asked him to do likewise. I then spread my arms all the way open out to my sides, palms facing him. Rob complied by moving his hands about three inches apart.

Obstacles Do Not Block The Path They Are The Path – Enjoy All

He said, 'That's it'. That's as far as I can go. His hands were not even separated as far apart as the width of his body but remained pretty much centered in front of his chest. I returned to the starting position and again asked him to do what I did. The result was the same numerous times.

During the process, I made it fun and funny. Never, however, was any of the humor at his expense. I wanted him to discover he could have fun stretching, no matter how much he stretched. I wanted it to be a positive, inspiring experience going through this process with me. I wanted to encourage and nurture him along.

It didn't matter to me whether or not he completed the task as I designed. The outcome I hoped for was that he would realize, some-time soon, that it was okay to stretch beyond his known boundaries and he could do it safely. I wanted him curious and willing to explore what he might someday soon be able to do. I emphasized implicitly and explicitly that he could sometime surprise himself with wonderful new feelings and behaviors that delighted him. I did this mostly by asking Directed Questions ™

Your Attitude Determines Your Altitude

And getting him to wonder and agree that it would be wonderful. I'd simply say things like, 'Wouldn't it be nice to discover how you can easily do new things that make you feel great?' 'Can you imagine how wonderful it would be to surprise and delight yourself in new and different ways?' I peppered my time with him with these types of questions that stimulated his imagination.

When we had finished Rob was able to move his hands 18 inches apart, at the furthest. I congratulated him. He took his seat and we continued with the rest of the training day. Later that night I got a call from the seminar sponsor. This gentleman asked me to come to his city and put on the seminar for people he gathered. Rob was his friend and was staying at his home.

Rob returned that night and when asked how the day went, he exclaimed loudly and emphatically, spreading his arms all the way out both sides, 'Rex tried to fix me but it didn't work!' The seminar sponsor called me a short while later overjoyed. He said Rob realized what he did and laughed hysterically. Having been his friend for many years he knew this was way beyond Rob's normal behavior and expression. Of course, I was delighted.

Every Champion Was Once A Contender Who Didn't Give Up

The next day Rob came into the workshop a completely different person. He carried himself differently. He spoke differently. He gestured with more confidence. He smiled. He was on his way to moving and being and living with greater ease. He was relaxed. He wasn't a top motivational speaker. He was an easy-going and more expressive individual.

When he left the seminar training, he was nowhere near ready to be a professional public speaker. Still, he had broken through a limitation and a way of life for himself going back years and years. Rob stayed in touch. He developed more confidence and more expressiveness. He was transformed. Later, he joined a speaking group and began to pursue his once secret dream.

Winners Fail But They Don't Quit

The power of the mind to make changes is remarkable. It just needs to be focused and directed and told what to do. You can overcome limitations in your thinking and your feeling and your behaving when you first learn to manage your thinking. As Henry Ford said, 'Whether you think you can or you think you can't you are right.'

You need to have faith in yourself to be able to resolve or handle any difficulty that arises in life. Plus, you're much better served if you consider anything in life that arises as a blessing. A challenge is an opportunity. You can move past whatever held you back and begin to move into a new way of being. You can <u>create</u> a <u>future</u> and <u>opportunity</u> for you <u>to excel</u>.

Take it gently. Nurture and encourage yourself. Have fun and delight. Develop a sense of humor and begin to wonder how much more fun and delight you can stand. Wouldn't it be marvelous to change with ease and joy? Wouldn't it be great to imagine this daily and find that you're smiling more throughout the day? You can, you know.

The Way We Spend Our Time Defines Who We Are

When things don't work out fast I think, "Perhaps, I need to LEARN MORE PATIENCE while pursuing my goal". The two concepts are not mutually exclusive. One can BE PATIENT and continue to act on one's behalf. Some people haven't learned this. Maybe, it is time to.

When things are troublesome or downright tough, we can learn to BE PERSISTENT or learn the ability to be joyful, anyway. When money is tight and debt looms, we learn to think and FOCUS ON ABUNDANCE instead. You learn to concentrate where it is important and how to focus your energy.

I am not saying there is a god ordaining this or a design to this. There very well may be, but that part doesn't matter. It is through trials we <u>become</u> <u>stronger</u> and well seasoned. We get more back than we could ever imagine. So, I say bring it! I want to learn.

Sales people who have <u>great</u> <u>success</u> right from the get-go, tremendous beginners luck, often hit great walls down the road. They go into major slumps. Why is this? Because of their early success, they only learned and used and practiced one way to sell.

They were 'lucky' and didn't encounter resistance. Therefore, they didn't learn how else to communicate and sell. They didn't learn how to <u>overcome</u> multiple objections. So later, when they get objections, they don't know what to do. They think their luck has turned.

Time Teaches Us How To Live

Many give up or they start learning to be better salespeople from then on. Overcoming problems helps us to develop other contingency programs. It helps us develop <u>positive</u> mindsets, behaviors and strategies to stay flexible and <u>overcome</u> other problems. The more we practice this, the better we get at it.

A problem facing child stars is that everyone says 'Yes' to them. They are coddled and handled and fawned over. They are favored and preferred for as long as they earn money for the studios. When the show ends or they enter the gangly unattractive time of adolescence and the fawning and 'Yes' saying stops, they don't know what to do.

They grew up as a silver spoon child, often petulant and demanding. You can hardly blame them. They never knew anything else. They didn't <u>learn</u> <u>how</u> <u>to</u> <u>successfully</u> <u>deal</u> <u>with</u> <u>people</u> or what to do when they don't get their way. They didn't learn win/win. You can win and the other person can win too.

Stay Focused

Adversity and delays provide us the time <u>needed</u> to develop as people and develop our skills and abilities. We fashion our mindset by having to maintain it positively even while things don't appear to be working in our favor. We learn how to stay the course and navigate difficult waters.

We LEARN PATIENCE, FAITH, TRUST and much more, when things take longer. If it is, "Wham, bam, thank you"... it just isn't as satisfying in the long run. Immediate results don't always benefit us overall. We live life while waiting for the seeds we planted to sprout in our garden.

Responsibility Is Liberating

Life continues on whether or not we are stuck or moving. We need to exercise our focus and keep our attention on what we want, even when it doesn't seem to be happening. We need to stay optimistic, cheerful and enthused. We stay carefree and lighthearted knowing all will work out for the good, eventually. We build many character muscles this way. We can improve in many different dimensions.

I want to improve. I want to get better at what I have learned to do. I want mastery, not accidental results. I want to LEARN TO STICK IT OUT AND MAKE IT HAPPEN and live the utmost! I don't merely want to escape what is, I want to rule what is. Don't you?

I have noticed that I am better off and far happier because things didn't manifest how or when I had hoped. I have become aware that I am far more delighted and well off because I went through some tough, or long, times without a quick remedy.

You Are Where Your Thoughts Have Brought You

I have learned to be happy without regard to what is going on. Things can be tough or easy and that doesn't change my happiness. It isn't acquisition of money, things or people that make me happy; but since I am happy, I seem to be able to acquire, and appreciate, those even more. Happiness first, is what time has helped me to be. Happiness first and then all else can follow!

Time is not the enemy some people think it is. It can be a wonderful and useful friend. Wine improves. People enjoy aged cheese and steak. We can get smarter and wiser and improve in time, too. Learn to embrace it. Learn to embrace all things and life becomes much more wonderful. Time gives you more opportunities than you can ever imagine. Become aware. Seek and you will find them. Meanwhile, celebrate everything!

Have a wonderful day!

"If you are not willing to risk the unusual, you will have to settle for the ordinary."
— *Jim Rohn*

"Be like a postage stamp. Stick with it until you get there."
— *Bob Proctor*

"Never say money is hard to get. Money will hear you and that's just what she will be."
— *Rev. Ike*

"What others think about you is none of your business."
— *Jack Canfield*

"Life's managed, not cured."
— *Phillip C. McGraw*

CHAPTER TWENTY-THREE

The Challenge That Can Easily Transform How You Think And Live

Would you do something that could MAKE A REAL DIFFER-ENCE for you in your life? Are you up for a challenge? It will help you create concentration, focus, energy and momentum. Well, are you? It's completely up to you.

If yes, then decide on a positive affirmation or a mantra. You know, a declaration, a positive assertion, something simple, something short. Make it a positive phrase that makes you <u>feel</u> <u>great</u> and go "oh yeah," when you say it or think it. See examples below.

Make sure to pick a powerful, juicy one for yourself. One that you <u>believe</u> is possible; one YOU BELIEVE you can have. Pick the <u>best</u> one you can think of that makes you FEEL MARVELOUS. Now, <u>commit</u> to saying it as many times as possible during day and night.

Energy Flows Where Your Attention Goes

When you get up, before you leave bed, say it 10, or 25 times. While brushing your teeth, shaving, showering, or otherwise occupied continue to focus on it and repeat it. While safely driving, any time you drive repeat it. THINK IT! SAY IT! FEEL IT! BELIEVE IT! BECOME IT! Shout it! Sing it! Love it!

Say it out loud with <u>great</u> enthusiasm as often as you can each day. Set a timer on your phone if you need a reminder. Before bed say it as much as you can prior to falling asleep. While with others, or at home or work, silently repeat it to yourself.

Do it again and again. <u>Commit</u> to no fewer than 7 days. If you really want to give it a powerful go, make it no fewer than 30 days. Pick one POWERFUL affirmation and recite it with POSITIVE FEELINGS as often as you can for at least the next seven to thirty days. You can also write it out each day. That helps reinforce it. Go for 90 days. Really put yourself into this! Only you will derive the benefits when you do.

You Become What You Think About

Concentrate on your one idea as often as you can. If, during this time, you become aware of thinking neutral or less than glorious thoughts, shift to your mantra. The goal is to constantly occupy your thoughts with it. Stop neutral or less than glorious thinking.

FEEL GREAT repeating your mantra. Emotions are what make the affirmations work. Merely reciting anything without emotion is practically meaningless. Put some real juice or 'oomph' into this. The military makes use of repetition and strong emotions.

During training troops chant, run, scream, holler and shout cadence. Cadence is rhythmic military songs chanted with powerful emotions. Not only do they chant with emotion, but, they utilize movement to accentuate it. They do cadence all the time, marching, jogging, walking. They combine the chanting with physical activity.

Laugh – Be Playful – Have Fun Creating – Be Joy Filled – Blissful

It's a powerful practice. It makes a number of troops into a cohesive unit. The same happens within you. It consolidates your resources and attention and helps you develop laser-like focus and concentration. You ALIGN YOUR INNER RESOURCES and become congruent. You become an 'army of one!' If they can use this, you can too!

You impress this affirmation on your subconscious. You want to GRAB HOLD OF THIS POSITIVE MESSAGE and 'get it'. You deliver this message by repeating it as often as you can with positive emotions. Keep at it. Your subconscious can and will get it.

What You Focus On Expands

Choose an affirmation that makes you <u>feel</u> great. Such as, "I am awesome". "I am unstoppable". "I am powerful". "I feel confident". "I easily clean the house." "It is easy to find ways to make extra money". "I am able to look people in the eye when speaking with them".

"I feel marvelous." "I can eat healthy foods and feel great." "I can grow my business." "I am healthy." "I am rich in many ways". "I have plenty of money". "I am invincible!" <u>Create</u> your own. Make sure you <u>feel</u> <u>it</u> <u>positively</u> and you honestly <u>believe</u> it. Start with that in mind. Other example of affirmations can be found back in chapters 4 and 7.

To make this image incredibly powerful, <u>imagine</u> yourself, <u>see</u> yourself, <u>already</u> being or doing or having the <u>good</u> you desire. Take time to VISUALIZE WHILE YOU CHANT YOUR AFFIRMATION. Spend at least five or more minutes. I do it everywhere. One of the more novel places I do it is while on the treadmill at the gym. I set a comfortable walking pace, hold on, close my eyes and do it.

I walk and hold on so I am safe. Then I <u>imagine</u> what I want while I repeat the mantra to myself. If I am on the treadmill for an hour, I exercised my mind and my body for an hour. I enjoy doing this. I also do it with eyes open on the treadmill and vary the speeds.

What You Think About You Bring About

I have even recorded myself speaking affirmations powerfully and positively onto my phone. Then while walking outside or on the treadmill, I play it and think along with it. I say it with emotion inside my mind.

When I record the affirmations I record it in first person. "I am magnificent!' Then I say, "You are magnificent". I also say it using my proper name as if one of my parents were speaking to me. "Rex Steven Sikes you are magnificent!" So I record it in first, second and third person. You can do this too if you want to. Then I play this recording while going to sleep and let it play all night long.

Do it for no less than seven days. Honestly, <u>commit</u> to it. There is much you can <u>discover</u> about yourself by putting this into practice. You may be quite amazed. FEEL FREE to keep it going longer. Become attuned or aware of new possibilities while taking this challenge. I say, go for 90. Still, it is up to you.

Research indicated years ago, the least amount of time it takes, using spaced repetition, consistently, for any practice to begin to become a habit, is 21 days. That means if you do anything routinely and consistently, for 21 days you are on your way to <u>beginning</u> to create a new habit. Ya ain't done yet, but you are on your way! Consider this.

What You Say Is What You Get

If, after a while, or a few days, you feel like tweaking your mantra go ahead. If you feel you'd be better off changing it to one you believe much more or feel better about, go ahead. Make whatever adjustment you need to make it stronger. Begin the challenge over from that point.

Think it as often as you can. SEE IT. SPEAK IT. DECLARE IT. FEEL GOOD. Fill as much time as you can with this thought and positive feelings over the seven days, 30 or 90 days. <u>Stay</u> <u>open</u> to discovery! Enjoy it! You will!

Have a great time and celebrate everything!

Delight in all your moments today! How much wonder and amazement can you find to enjoy!

"If you really want the key to success, start by doing the opposite of what everyone else is doing."
—— Brad Szollose

CHAPTER TWENTY-FOUR

Why, And What To Do, When The Poo Hits The Propeller

Okay, you saw the movie *The Secret*. You practice the Law Of Attraction. You maintained a positive attitude and things got worse. WTF? Why on Earth should things turn sour? 'It's not fair', you might exclaim.

Yes, you may be doing many things right. You have tried different practices. You have maintained them for a while. Perhaps, you would say, "I've tried everything but nothing works!"

Let's pretend there is a god or a source or an intelligence that governs the universe and its laws. Imagine this infinite source of wisdom and benevolence.

Hardship Prepares People For An Extraordinary Destiny

IMAGINE this source is actually you but you have, long ago, forgotten this about yourself. You pretend, in so many ways, to be limited and have issues. Just pretend again, for a moment, and accept the premise as possible. It is a hypothetical exercise. Try it on.

You have all this INCREDIBLE POWER and wisdom to tap into but you don't and you haven't. Instead you bought into everything that was told to you, and modeled for you, while you were growing up and getting older.

Instead of living from your source of power you live from limitation and lack. Not completely, sometimes things are great, sometimes not. Things are the way they are. You like, and you don't at times. Life is okay.

You want more. You decide you will PRACTICE POSITIVE THINKING and related disciplines. You begin and you expect the best. Lo and behold, the fan gets covered with crap, and you thought you'd be free of it.

Hardship Comes From Outside Failure From Inside

This is the experience of many people. Why? Because they think if they just think right everything will magically change and they won't actually have to do anything at all. They hope, wish, and pray.

That inner you, that wiser infinite source, knows you could be handed everything on a platter, or you could evolve and learn and make things happen, by getting back in touch with what makes you powerful.

In order for you to TAP INTO YOUR HIGHER SELF you need to be challenged so you will seek yourself. Otherwise, you won't. Most people don't pray unless times get bad and then they become the consummate beggar.

God Gives His Toughest Battles To His Strongest Soldiers

They plead that things change miraculously for them, hoping, wishing, doubting, but pleading, "Pleaseeeeee! I promise I will be good!" They put their faith and requests outside of themselves.

They totally miss the possibility to change. They think it is from outside! Somehow, things will come to them if they think right or do right. That is why most people miss the boat on the LOA. They THINK of themselves separate from the source of their problems and SOLUTIONS.

People want to be spared the hardship. They want to avoid trials and tribulations. They want the cozy, cushy, lush, LAVISH GOOD LIFE dropped in their lap.

The Biggest Obstacles In Life Are The Barriers Our Mind Creates

If you want to get to the top of Everest you have to do the climbing. If you want to win the race you have to be dedicated to finishing, and finishing first. That is the law, mindset and action. KEEP GOING and never give up. See it through to the end. Persist! You must PERSIST no matter what.

You get challenged because you <u>are</u> bigger than you think you are. Your limited mind isn't aware of it so you need to <u>become convinced</u>. You need to be tested by fire and made aware of what YOU ARE CAPABLE of. You need to <u>learn who you are</u>. So things turn crappy so <u>you</u> can find out. Steel is forged by fire. Diamonds made by pressure. You are too!

This is precisely when you must APPLY YOUR POSITIVE ATTI-TUDE. You must persist and maintain your course. However, this is the exact same time, many throw in the towel. Then, complain that nothing they tried works. Nothing you try, will work. It is <u>YOU</u> who works or doesn't.

Obstacles Are Those Frightful Things You See...

When you expect the Law Of Attraction or someone, or something else, to come to your aid and miraculously save you, or SOLVE YOUR PROBLEMS, you are missing YOU. You are putting your faith in magic instead of putting faith in your infinite talents and wisdom and abilities where it belongs.

You <u>are</u> the creator and you create these tests, so you could find yourself again. It is the quest. The journey. The challenges are there for you to prove yourself, to find yourself. In adversity is <u>opportunity</u>. Find it!

It is all about you. Struggles come. Learn from them. RISE ABOVE THEM. Accept the challenge. LEARN TO LAUGH in the face of difficulty. You are either bigger than the problems or they are bigger than you. Which it is determines how you live and what you get or don't get. You are bigger than any obstacle. Never forget that! Always remember, you are bigger than any obstacle!

... When You Take Your Eyes Off Your Goal

The opportunity is for you to come into your own <u>incredible</u> power. This is for you to FIND YOURSELF, or even better, to create yourself. Many will quit and claim the LOA doesn't work. That's too bad for them. And it's too bad for you, if you do that. If you can't find and, remember, your inner greatness, then you miss out. You need to own your power. Claim it! Own It. Embrace It! Live it!

You find it from challenge not from cozy, comfort where everything comes to you from the outside. Can you create cozy comfort? Sure, but not without learning how to navigate all the woes first. You move through the negative to the positive because that IS how it works. You overcome and you win!

When You Face Your Struggles, You Overcome Them

You become a champion by contest. You win by playing <u>and</u> finishing the game well. If you wimp out, you are finished. If you see it through to the end, <u>you</u> can <u>win</u> the prize.

Life is whatever it is. Easy or hard, accept it. Get over it. And get on with it. Understand 'shit' happens, for you to rise above it. Learn there isn't anything you can't handle or you can't do if you put your mind to it. You are bigger than any obstacle! Act like it! Own It! Claim your positive power! Live it! Live IT!

We Grow When We Face Challenges Not When It Is Easy

Some people want to claim the goods without the effort. The effort is your evidence. When you SUCCESSFULLY NAVIGATE THE TOUGHEST TIMES, you <u>discover</u> what you are made of and what you can do. Otherwise, it is only theory. You are the proof.

Without the tough times you have no evidence. Once you do, you can be confident you can handle anything. You KNOW YOUR POWER. You are secure in your abilities. You realize you are a powerful, positive creator and attractor. There is no doubt. You have come home to yourself and who you are.

This is what so many people, perhaps most people, don't understand about pursuing your goals and making your dreams come true.

Success Is The Sum Of Small Efforts Repeated Daily

Whenever troubled, learn to smile and to laugh. Let nothing stop you. Develop the attitude that YOU CAN HANDLE ANYTHING that comes your way and you will. Appreciate it all and celebrate everything!

I always emphasize how simple it is to make positive changes and succeed. Whether you want to accelerate your career, improve your bank account, enjoy a delightful relationship or celebrate more of what life has to offer, it is easy once you know how.

I am going to give you a few quotes from Robert Collier, one of the early New Thought leaders to, again, drive that point home for you. Collier lived from 1885 to 1950. He wrote, "You can do anything you wish to do, have anything you wish to have, be anything you wish to be." What follows are a few more of Robert's words:

"Visualize this thing you want. SEE IT, FEEL IT, believe in it. Make your mental blueprint and begin to build."

Now Is The Only Time There Is

"Any thought that is passed on to the subconscious often enough and convincingly enough is finally accepted."

"See things as you would have them be instead of as they are."

"Success is the sum of small efforts, repeated day in and day out."

"The great successful men of the world have used their imagination; they think ahead and create their mental picture in all its details, filling in here, adding a little there, altering this a bit and that a bit, but steadily building, steadily building."

"The first essential, of course, is to know what you want."

Learn Naturally As A Child Learns Naturally

"All power is from within and is therefore under our own control."

"Desire is the planting of your seed. Very few persons, comparatively, know how to Desire with sufficient intensity. They do not know what it is to feel and manifest that intense, eager, longing, craving, insistent, demanding, ravenous Desire which is akin to the persistent, insistent, ardent, overwhelming Desire of the drowning man for a breath of air; of the shipwrecked or desert-lost man for a drink of water; of the famished man for bread and meat…"

Well, there you have it. I think it is more than sufficiently self-explanatory. I want to only remind you of one quote again in particular, so that it is not overlooked. All are great, of course, but it is this one.

Repetition Is The Way You Learn And Create Habits

"Success is the sum of small efforts, repeated day in and day out." It is the small things we do on a consistent and persistent basis that make all the difference in the world. Walking the same way through the valley floor creates a pathway. It is the continuous repetition that creates the path.

Some people encourage massive action. That is fine as long as it is sustainable. However, often it is not and people quit. That is unfortunate because there is this other way. Make small positive efforts daily. Build your success habits bit by bit. MAKE IT FUN AND ENJOYABLE. Don't overwhelm or exert yourself. Don't run out of steam. Eat an elephant one bite at a time.

You Understand These Lessons At A Variety Of Levels

We are exposed to and <u>learn</u> new things. Through repeated practice we can <u>build</u> new habits, which can <u>replace</u> the old ones. Our brains literally <u>evolve</u>. We <u>create</u> new neural pathways. We lay down <u>new</u> mental tracks that become <u>reliable</u>. Neurons that fire together, <u>do</u> wire together.

Never give up. Do small things. Do a little bit each day, and you will make <u>progress</u> to your goal. Whatever that is. YOU CAN BE, DO AND HAVE anything you want. ANYTHING YOU WANT! Napoleon Hill, reminded us, "<u>Whatever</u> the mind can conceive, <u>and</u> believe, we <u>can</u> achieve".

Stay Open Stay Teachable – Empty Your Cup – Let Go - Learn

Keep in mind, if you make just 1% improvement each day, in a year you will have improved 365%. That can be a huge transformation. Drop by drop the tub gets filled. Little by little you can <u>accomplish</u> big things.

Since ALL POWER IS FROM WITHIN and therefore under your control keep the faith, never give up. Do the little things, consistently, and you get what you want. Keep making your dreams a reality. It can be easier than you ever thought and it is much simpler! Celebrate and delight! In how many different ways can you amaze and delight yourself?

"Your positive action combined with your positive thinking results in success."
—— *Shiv Khera*

"You and your purpose in life are the same thing. Your purpose is to be you."
—— *George Alexiou*

239

CHAPTER TWENTY-FIVE

How You Really Make Changes: NO BS!

Do you want to know how to MAKE LASTING CHANGES? No BS just the cold, hard, bare-naked truth! Do you want that? Can you handle the truth? We shall see. We shall see. Would you like your life to be positively different and better? Are you committed to making it so?

Many people want things but don't commit to doing what is necessary or commit to having them. They hope a lot. Mostly, they whine a lot. Is this you? How do you spend your time? How do you spend your thinking time and feeling time most of each day?

Does it work for you or against you? If it isn't working for you, if it isn't supporting you in being who you want to be, and having what you want to have; then it is not a good use of your time. If it isn't supportive, it is unsupportive. If it isn't living and growing, it's dying.

You Create Your Own Destiny Even If You Don't Take Control

DO YOU UNDERSTAND THIS? THIS IS CRUCIAL TO GET! You need to absorb it. You need to embrace and embody these concepts. If you are not doing what you want YOU are not creating what you want. YOU are actively and passively keeping it all the same!

WHAT are YOU Doing? It is important to stop and take notice. What on earth are you doing for YOU? Now is not the time to whine, blame, complain, or excuse. NOW is the time to DECIDE to make the necessary changes to have what you want.

If you don't, you won't. That is truth, plain and simple, cold and hard. No BS. Either you do it or you don't. If you don't, don't expect anything TO CHANGE. If you change what you are currently doing, then you can change the results you are getting and begin to <u>get results</u> that you want.

THIS IS CRUCIAL! YOU HAVE TO READ THIS AGAIN AND AGAIN

To make my point I'll used the condemned house analogy. People complain about the house. They find what is wrong. Then they spend the bulk of their time worrying about it, complaining about it, and blaming whom or whatever for it. They make excuses.

The story they tell, their thoughts, feelings and what they say are less than glorious. They are negative and downers preoccupied by the condemned house. All they see is what is wrong. Their predominant thoughts, most all of their time, is what they do not want. STOP! Don't be like them! Stop! <u>Be different!</u>

In order to have a new house you must turn your attention to what you want the new house to be and then work to build it. Get it? The predominant thoughts you should have are <u>how incredible</u> the new house will be. You need to envision living in the new house. Feel it.

If You Do Nothing – Nothing Will Be The Future You Have

They need to plan to build it. Make a blueprint. Assemble whomever. Raise the money and the resources and build the house. No time should be wasted complaining about what was. All time should be spent making happen what will be. Do you get this?

Many people don't. They read it. They hear it. Still, they focus on what they don't want. WHY? Habit. That is what they learned to do. So, that is what they continue to do. How long? Forever! Until, they decide to change their habits and take charge.

<u>If you don't decide</u>, you will continue to do what you have always done, chronically and habitually. You can hope and wish and pray for a change and nothing will change until you change it. YOU must INITIATE THE CHANGES. You must do it. How? You ask.

I have repeatedly shared how in these pages, and in my blog posts, in workshops, seminars, in interviews and discussions. To begin you make the decision that YOU WILL CHANGE. COMMIT TO CHANGING for the better. Take baby steps. If nothing else, do just enough daily to make a little bit of difference.

If You Think You Can Or You Think You Can't You Are Right

Eventually, you will do more. Change may be gradual. Most likely it will be, but it can also be instantaneous. What it is and for whom shouldn't matter. Simply commit! Make yourself and your life the best. Read, study and apply. If you don't do, nothing will change.

You can read all about building houses. You can talk about it forever. Unless, you TAKE ACTION and begin working a plan and begin building the house, it will remain only a possibility. You make it a reality. You gather your inner and outer resources and YOU MAKE IT HAPPEN. Once your mindset is correct you apply the 2%.

YOU CREATE and YOU ATTRACT. When your mind is set and you are absolutely determined, let nothing stop you. Adjust and adapt until you get what you want or something better. It is not fate. It is YOU who shapes your own destiny. YOU make it happen! Get it?

Action Is The Proper Fruit Of Knowledge

If you don't you are doomed to repeat the endless habitual cycle of wanting but not having until you change it. Until you take action and step up to the plate. Until you DO IT, it is only an idea. Thoughts become things because we translate them from an idea to the tangible.

How many times have you been asked this before? How often have you had a brilliant idea but did not act on it? Later, you discovered someone else had the same or similar idea but is now making money hand over fist because they put it into action. They made it reality.

Now their reality is rich, while your reality is whining about what could have been. "If only, …" is how many people live out their regrets. Had you acted back then, today it would all be different. Have you ever thought or done this?

To Know And Not To Do – Is To Not Know

I have done this numerous times. I have seen others take my work and spread it world wide making millions because my work, works! I didn't. They did. They got the money! They got the fame and the credit for it.

It sucks. BUT it is water over the dam. No use complaining. At the same time it is awesome! People are using my methods to make permanent, positive change all over the world, whether they got it from me or someone else. WOW, how cool is that! My work works and lives are transformed. Had I acted, yes they would have gotten it from me.

Have you missed an opportunity to put an idea of yours into action? Most of us have, it is true. I point this out because we are all very similar. We all do or don't do things. We are in the same boat in life. If these others can do it, so can we. If I can, so can you. If you can, so can I.

The More You Do The More You Can Do – Skill Comes Of Doing

Get it? Do you understand? If not yet, how soon do you suppose you will begin to decide to make a real difference for yourself? Are you going to MAKE POSITIVE CHANGES or sadly remain the same? It is all up to you. How soon will you DECIDE TO BE DIFFERENT and TAKE CHARGE?

I wonder. Maybe you should wonder, too!

If you do really get it, start now to make a real difference for yourself and your future. Read, study and APPLY. Apply what you are in the process of learning! Application of your knowledge is the most crucial piece. Without doing, there is no new being or having. Understand?

Take charge. Determine what you want and GO FOR IT! Put it immediately to use. You don't have to know how yet, just decide what you want and that you will have it.

You will FIND OR CREATE A WAY eventually. Go as far as you can see and when you get there, you can see farther. There will be no stopping you. If it is good and positive for all, go for it!

The Future You Live Is The One You Make Happen Or Don't

Be thankful that you can. Appreciate where you are and where you have come from. BE GRATEFUL for the hard learning lessons and the easy times too. FEEL POSITIVE about back then, now and your future. Take time to really feel it. DELIGHT, give thanks and celebrate everything!

Maybe you should go ahead and gift this book to others! Share the ideas and concepts. Help others transform their lives. That would be a great way to make today count. Feed it forward! Feel fantastic!

How many different ways can you think to apply what you are learning from this book?

"It's really important that we throw these false beliefs into the dustbin."
— *Anik Singal*

"Open your eyes to the beauty around you; open your mind to the wonders around you; open your heart to those who love you; and always be true to yourself. "
— *Donna Davis*

CHAPTER TWENTY-SIX

How To Manifest And Get It All From The Universe

Do you want to live the good life? Do you want more money? Would you like more passion and romance? How about more family connection? How would you like the career of your dreams? Want more leisure time? Want to know how to attract good things?

If you want it, you can have it. Thought leaders from the dawn of time have been explicitly and implicitly telling us that we can. There has been lots of misunderstanding, even attempts to obfuscate the methods. I have written for years on these subjects and this book has delved into them in them as a basic formula.

Simply reading this book can help you transform. However, if you really want it to make great things happen then you must do more than just that, because reading is not enough. Study this book. You'll learn to create and attract what you want.

If You Can See It In Your Mind – You Can Hold It In Your Hand

I recommend re-reading it many times. Most importantly, you must TAKE ACTION. If you don't do what you are told, you won't benefit. To know and not to do is to not know. Action is the proper fruit of knowledge.

Knowing is not enough. Reading one more book won't help. This book is sufficient for your transformation. You create and attract by taking action. You don't expect your bed to be made or your food to spontaneously appear, do you? I bet you don't.

You make your bed or your food. You make your dreams come true as well. You attract people to you by the kind of person you are. If you are nice, kind, appealing, or friendly you attract others and/or are attracted to others for various reasons. This is important to get.

You don't get anything for nothing. You must have some skin in the game. You transfer money to the grocer to purchase goods. There is a medium of exchange. You hand over cash, check or credit which is money or energy and take the groceries. Exchange. You exchange.

Take Charge Of Your Life – Make What You Want Happen

One form of energy for another is exchanged. I say 'energy' because everything is energy, after all. If you don't pay you don't play, or get. If you rob others you will pay in a different fashion, with your time, if you are caught. Or perhaps, you pay for it in other 'karmic' ways. The bottom line is there is an action exchange.

To manifest and attract you must follow the formula as laid out. 1. Know what you specifically want and focus. 2. Concentrate on and affirm it as already yours. Become passionate about it. 3. Desire it positively and strongly. 4. Believe you will get it to the point of certainty. 5. Take action to get it and don't give up. 6. Persist until it is yours, adjusting as necessary along the way. Put all your energies into making it happen.

You affirm, visualize, 'act as if,' to organize your mental, emotional and physical, even spiritual resources, to align yourself so you are aimed at making it happen. You are congruent inside and out. You are of one accord. You are driven by purpose. You are a "go-getter," You are an "army of one!"

Energy Flows Where Your Attention Goes

YOU make it happen. It doesn't happen for you by magic. You transform yourself into someone who gets one's goals AS IF by magic. It can seem magical and to an extent it actually is. Still, you aren't locked in a cave waving a wand and goods appear. Get it?

When you are congruently aligned and dedicated to making your purpose happen you vibrate differently. Your energies are alive and enthused. Because of this you attract. You attract people and events and circumstances. Here is why.

You become attuned to opportunities. Remember, your brain finds you <u>positive</u> opportunity because you have tuned it to look for these. You find circumstances and events you might have otherwise missed because your personal radar is sensitized to discover these. It seems magical.

This Moment – How You Feel Is Creating Your Future

It is magical in that your entire being is seeking <u>positive</u> experiences. You raise your positive energy. Your attitude and outlook are positive. Others of like mind and energy are attracted to you, as moths are to a flame. You evolve yourself into an attracting energy.

You manifest by creating and attracting. You engage in both. Ready for the last step? Step 7. <u>YOU</u> step aside. <u>You</u> get out of the way. <u>You</u> allow it to happen. <u>You</u> open up to receive it all. Many people screw up getting because they never finish pursuing. They keep pushing and pushing! They keep wanting!

You pay the grocer and then you receive the goods. You don't force your money on the grocer. You give it. You put an order in at a restaurant and then you expectantly wait for your food to come. You don't cook it or micro-manage the chef. You <u>wait</u> and <u>allow</u> them to bring it. You ordered it now you <u>receive</u> it.

Who You Become Is The Person You Decide To Be

The attitude is one of expectancy. You attract and then you make room for it to happen. You do and then you <u>allow</u> the results. You work or play during the day and you sleep at night. You let go and rest. You eat and allow your body to process it. It will do it.

You aren't giving up. You aren't quitting. You are expecting. You know it is coming. You aren't worried or fearful or anxious. You don't fret. You are <u>confident</u>. You know and are <u>certain</u> it is yours. You allow it. Even though you make it happen you still <u>allow the results</u>. Get it?

Some people give and give and give and give. Have you noticed? Some of them aren't very good at allowing you to give to them. They are not good receivers. In order to get from the universe you make it happen and you let it happen. You need to be a good giver and a good receiver. You allow the energies to exchange. It is a two-way street.

Life Never Asked You To Struggle It Responds To Your Mood

Some readers may be poor givers. They don't start or go after their dreams. They wait and wish. Others may push and push but don't relax into trusting and allowing it. You must do both. Attitude is everything. <u>Trust</u> and <u>be</u> <u>certain</u>. Both action and rest are required!

There are rhythms and cycles. Day turns into night. Tides come and go. Seasons change. We sow and reap at different times. Learning to go with the flow means you do or don't do depending on what cycle you are in. You go with it. You trust it. You allow it because you made it.

<u>You</u> did the work, now <u>you</u> reap the results. Trust. Attitude is everything! Allow. If you did the work, allow the results. If you didn't do the work then do it to get the rewards. Once you have done it, let it happen. You are not quitting. You are adjusting.

We Receive What We Expect To Receive – Trust And Allow

When you plant a seed you do the work planting. You don't grow the seed. Growing is the seed's and nature's responsibility. SO you have to know your part in the process. You plant and you reap. Get it? The results all come about as a result of planting. You don't control the results but you do control your efforts.

Accept the results and if they aren't to your liking, <u>adjust</u> that too. If they aren't as good as you hoped, be <u>grateful</u> for what they are, <u>adjust</u> your attitude, and be <u>flexible</u> to do whatever is required to get better results. Sometimes, things just aren't as great as we hope they will be. Get up. Get over it. Put a <u>smile</u> on your lips. Adjust and <u>move</u> forward. Be grateful and <u>celebrate</u> everything!

BUT also, be open to the possibility that the results may blow you away. They could go beyond anything you imagined. Allow for <u>anything</u>! That's why some affirm by saying, "This or something better." Since you can't know how things turn out also be ready to be delighted. You can be delightfully surprised. Allow for it. Don't be a tight ass about manifesting. Create some space for surprises.

Gratitude Is The Open Doorway To Overflowing Abundance

Gratitude is marvelous. If you did nothing but were genuinely happy and thankful, feeling blessed about everything in your life you'd amaze yourself. It would be <u>magnificent</u>. Even if it weren't, you wouldn't care because you'd be too filled with <u>bliss</u> feeling glad about it. Right?

True, genuine, heartfelt appreciation for your challenges and struggles and for whatever you have and for whoever is in your life, difficult or easy, changes everything into potential, positive benefit. Live with genuine gratitude and your life will be filled with all manner of good things.

You'd be in heaven on earth. Try it on. Do it. Exclaim, "I love my life!" Then let the universe know you are willing to accept any magic and miracles that come your way this day. Go ahead and say that too. Smile and delight. Become an excellent receiver. Celebrate everything!

Allow yourself a lot of delight today!

> *"Don't wish it was easier, wish you were better. Don't wish for less problems, wish for more skills. Don't wish for less challenge, wish for more wisdom."*
> —— *Jim Rohn*

REVIEW

Time to review, to revisit. Time to state everything somewhat differently. Thoughts are things. What you think about you bring about. Napoleon Hill said, 'Whatever you can conceive, and believe, you can achieve.'

He stated, as have others, that our brains are broadcasting stations transmitting thoughts. Every thought transmitted is a vibration. Remember, like attracts like. When you look in the mirror, who you are is reflected back. Whatever you transmit is reflected or attracted back to you.

The speed at which you attract or manifest depends on three things. The first is the intensity with which you think and transmit. How powerful and emotionally charged it is? The second is the frequency of your transmission. How often are you thinking and feeling it? Third, is there any resistance?

You Are What You Think About – What You Focus On Expands

Remember, your subconscious serves you and only says "Yes." If your subconscious beliefs run counter to what you want, you create resistance. Your subconscious continues to do the old, chronic, habitual thinking in order to keep you safe and the same.

In order to change you need to get out of your comfort zone. You need to minimize the resistance. You do that by letting go of your limiting beliefs. Becoming aware of when you are stuck. Then changing it. That means you exercise awareness and conscious choice. You decide to be different.

That is the purpose for doing those belief exercises. Remember, you want to become aware of those beliefs that hold you back so you can drop them, thereby minimizing or eliminating resistance.

The Mirror Reflects Back Who You Are – Like Attracts Like

The Law of Attraction, just like gravity, works whether you are conscious of it or not. You either work with it or you don't. When pilots fly planes, gravity doesn't stop. They apply other principles and laws to work with it to get the plane to take flight. You work with the laws of attraction and cause and effect and other laws to get more of what you want.

I am sharing how you work with it. Only you can create your reality. Only you can get your results. Every thought and feeling you have is a vibration <u>you</u> are transmitting. If some of your transmissions are positive, but most of them not so positive, you get mixed or less than glorious results. This is why you devote your energy to make yourself feel good. Think positive most of the time.

The goal is to <u>feel</u> <u>your</u> <u>best</u> most of the time. Actually, when you consider it, anything you want, a romance, a car, a watch, a job, a house is to provide you certain feelings. Otherwise, why do you want it? Obviously, you want these things because you think you will feel good when you have them. Get it?

The Goal Is To Feel Good - Feel Your Best Most Of The Time.

If something comes along that is tragic, what to do? You lose your job, your house or car, a loved one dies, are you supposed to feel blissful? No, the goal is to <u>feel</u> <u>the</u> <u>best</u> <u>you</u> <u>can</u>. It would be unrealistic to assume you could leap from great sorrow to bliss, but you can inch by inch, bit by bit. Step by step you work toward feeling a bit better. You work at feeling the best you can. Get it?

Still, in general, you want to feel as good as possible <u>as</u> <u>much</u> <u>of</u> <u>the</u> <u>time</u> as you can. You attract back what you are putting out there. You attract back what you vibrate or transmit. So make it your daily routine to do things that make you <u>feel</u> <u>good</u>.

Read inspiring material. Listen to motivating audios. Hang around with positive people. Engage in physical activities that help you feel and think your best. Visualize, affirm and aim your mind and emotions. Take inspired actions.

Thoughts to Feelings To Actions To Results – Mindset Matters

Remember you must define, specify your goal and make it a burning, obsessive desire. You do this through affirming, visualization and repetition, for as long enough a duration of time, as is necessary. As it becomes a burning desire you simultaneously, begin to develop the belief and the certainty that you can and will get your goal. Make your goal a reality. Make your dream obsession come true.

To help do this you write your goal out specifically. Read it out loud at least twice a day. Affirm and visualize. Think about it. Remember, intensity plus frequency, minus resistance, determines the speed of you manifesting your desires.

Hill said, as you do this, you tap into 'Infinite Intelligence' or your vast subconscious storehouses and intuition. Pay attention to your inner voice and hunches. Your RAS is seeking opportunities based on what is important to you. Your goal or your DCP is what is most important to you.

Thoughts Become Words And Feelings

As you move forward remember to help others, celebrate others, give to others and go the extra mile in helping them. Develop an attitude of co-operation. You get back what you put out and you want to attract people, events and situations that are positive and beneficial to you. So you go first.

What you put out is attracted back. You attract back what you are. So don't be petty, competitive, or vindictive. Be a blessing to all. Remember you are always broadcasting or transmitting something. The question is what are you broadcasting most of the time? Whatever that is, determines what you get back. If you want the best, be the best first.

So you have defined you DCP and you have a burning desire for it. Now you affirm and repeat until you come to believe, with certainty, you can make it happen. During this process you will begin to get intuitive flashes and hunches to take inspired actions toward making it happen.

Change Your Thoughts And Your Words And Feelings Change

Here is a key. There are four levels of learning. 1) Unconscious Incompetence. That means you don't know, you don't know. For example, at one time you didn't know there were bikes you could ride.

At some point you become aware there were bikes, and that you couldn't ride it. When you realized this you became 2) Consciously Incompetent.

Then you try riding a bike and find it difficult and awkward. You, sort of, talk your way through it. You have so many things you have to pay attention to all at once and you can't yet do it smoothly. You don't know how but you are learning as you ride imperfectly. It is hit and miss much of the time.

Stay Open – Have Fun – Delight – Celebrate Everything

You aren't that good but with continual effort you get better and better. This is the level of 3) Conscious Competence. It is effort.

Then, one day, you got on your bike and road with glee. You could ride and think about other things. It was easy. You had become 4) Unconsciously Competent. Bike riding became a reliable, automatic skill and habit. You no longer had to think about how you were doing, or talk yourself through. Now you are able to ride with ease.

We go through the same levels learning how to attract and manifest our desires. Currently, you are somewhere between Conscious Incompetence and Conscious Competence. Some of you may be Unconsciously Competent.

Right now, in Conscious Competence, it seems a struggle. You sometimes manage to manifest while at other times you don't. It can be frustrating. Remember it is hit and miss. Just stick with it.

You Can Always Create Or Find A Way

Really, I mean, stick with it. Repeat the process over and over again for a long enough time and you'll become Unconsciously Competent. It will become a reliable, automatic habit. Your life will radically improve and you will manifest with great ease. Unconscious Competence is the domain of Mastery.

There are three ways you can define your definite chief purpose. 1) You can use great specificity. You can name make, model, brand and all the benefits and features of your favorite watch, car, boat, house or whatever it is you want. You know what you want, but leave the time frame open for when you get it.

You can specify all the terms and conditions you want and supply a deadline. That is being even more precise. "I want X and I want it by this date". 2) You can also, be more general. You can think, "I want a house that makes me feel incredible" but you don't specify the place, the size, the number of rooms etc. You just want a house that makes you feel great. You don't specify a date either. General, is okay, too.

If You Don't Like The Results You Get - Adjust And Continue

I suggest you be specific at first. It is good practice to be as precise as you can be. It helps you visualize and to know precisely what it is you are going after.

Lastly, number 3) You can simply go for the feeling. "I want to feel incredible". Remember, the number one goal is to feel the best you can, anyway. So the more you feel wonderful, the more wonderful things you can attract.

When you are vague you <u>allow</u> for surprises. You don't specify conditions but are willing to be surprised. You allow for unexpected good. Some people suggest you be very specific but add, 'this or something better' to the affirmation or DCP. This allows wiggle room to be blessed in ways you might never otherwise consider. You do want to remain open for unexpected good. I love this saying. "I will go through all my days carefree and lighthearted, knowing all is well". Everything all works out for the best.

You Create Every Single Moment Of Your Life

Start with feeling good because this is what you want most anyway. All things and activities are typically ways of attempting to feel good. So, <u>feel good now</u>. Aim at feeling good now. Make yourself feel good!

That is why you drop issues. That is why you let go of limiting beliefs. That is why you shift from the negative to the positive. You change your state from less than glorious <u>to</u> FEEL GOOD! Get it! You do anything and everything to feel good. SO go ahead and feel good. Do it! Battle over! You win! Get it?

The bottom line is, know what you want. Make it an obsession. DEVELOP the CERTAINTY <u>you will accomplish</u> it. Think about it and feel about it in positive, powerful, emotionally charged ways, frequently. Let go of anything else. Drop doubt, fear, worry and all the rest. Use the exercises and this book as your guide to eliminate resistance and move ahead. <u>Persist</u> at it until you get it. Keep going!

Take 100% Responsibility For Everything In Your Life

Another powerful method is to <u>FOCUS ON GRATITUDE</u>. Find the silver lining in every situation. Every problem can be reframed as an opportunity and a blessing. Seek solutions and keep your attention on the solution and off the problem. If you <u>consider everything a blessing</u> you let go of all the resistance. You are blessed.

You are fortunate. You are lucky. Celebrate everything! This is an incredible way to live.

Live, love, laugh, more and life will be magically, wonderful. Apply what you have learned, work on it playfully, not too seriously now. MASTER IT and you will have developed new powerful supportive habits that operate automatically. Life becomes a wonderful adventure.

From this point on continue to grow. Keep evolving. The goal is not the absence of problems but to become larger than your problems so that you can handle anything life brings your way. Whatever it brings, if you are bigger than the issue, and you consider the issue a blessing and an opportunity, you have become free! Remember you are bigger than any obstacle. You are truly blessed!

You have within you everything you need! I think that is a wonderful way to live. Godspeed.

The more you win the more you win. Success breeds more success. Have fun!

"The world around us is nothing more and nothing less than a mirror of what we have become from within." — *Gregg Braden*

AFTERWORD

Congratulations if you have read this far. You may have noticed principles, concepts and themes repeating. Repetition is necessary for mastery. You want to MASTER THESE PRINCIPLES and concepts. You want to master your thoughts, feelings, actions and behaviors. You want to BECOME UNCONSCIOUSLY COMPETENT. When you do a new world opens up for you.

Perhaps, you have already noticed things shifting. Perhaps, you are already feeling much better and manifesting much more of what you want. That is awesome, keep at it. If you haven't yet, hang in there. Everything happens in the right time, as long as you continue to persist, without giving up.

Whether you got little results or stellar results continue to study and re-read this book and apply what you are learning. Each time you go through it you will increase your awareness and abilities. The more you study and apply the more mastery you make happen. Mastery, after all, is an ongoing process.

See It – Declare It – Speak it – Make It Happen

Always remember it is you doing it. It is you applying the laws of cause and effect. It is you applying the laws of attraction. You create and you attract. This is the piece so many miss. They think it comes from outside of them.

It doesn't. It comes from within you. You already are everything. You already possess everything. You just need to journey in awareness to discover this and to have all of it become available. You discover who you truly are. From within to without. From heart to heart we attract each other. It is an inner process that can influence outer circumstances.

Some things you can do.

I mentioned some studies in the book but I am <u>not</u> sourcing them. I do this purposefully. If you are truly interested in transforming yourself, and you want the background, then do the legwork. Make that part of your study, as you study this material. You will <u>benefit</u> from looking deeper into things. You will benefit from not having it given to you.

So the research is part of your process, should you decide you want to look into it.

Make your dreams come true. Keep a journal of your successes. Do the exercises and make them a habit as well. Bit by bit. Drop by drop. Get it? I am sure if you haven't, that you one day will, so long as you continue to explore and adventure this way.

See It – Feel It – Speak it – Make It Happen

If you read this far I congratulate you. Here is one of the most <u>powerful</u> exercises you can do for yourself. I put it here to <u>reward</u> those who made it this far! Keep in mind that your habits and conditioning, your programming that you operate from, originates or comes from every thought you think, and every word you have ever spoken out loud. Thoughts are things.

Nothing is missing from you or your life. You are source. You are made of the same ingredients as is everything else and you are conscious. You are one with all. You are source. You already have everything. You, your conscious mind self, doesn't fully realize this, yet. So you continue wanting what you already are and what you already possess. This keeps it from showing up.

You don't think you have it yet. You want it. Wanting means not having, get it? So this exercise can really transform you. I heartily suggest you do it. Don't treat it lightly, do it deliberately. Go back and read the book over again. ANY time and any place you see the word want or desire in relation to your DCP, goal or dream change it. Use positive language and state it differently!

Change it to one of these variations. Instead of "I want," think and say "I choose." "I choose to have" "I am." "I choose to create." "I am interested in making ..." "I choose to make happen..." "I am making happen..." "I prefer to create..." "I will make happen..." "I feel like experiencing..." "I am claiming...." "I am manifesting." "I intend to create..." "It is my intention to..." Adjust the wording so it makes sense.

Bless Heal Prosper

Do you get why you do this? Instead of wanting it, choose to make it happen. Be deliberate. You are choosing this right now. This is your choice. You are deciding to make it happen. So re-read the book changing all the phrasing. Put a guard on your lips so you do this in everyday life as well. This exercise will help wire that in for you. This is incredibly powerful. Don't miss out. It will reveal to you how you already have what you have been wanting.

Other may have not read this far so they just won't know until someday they discover it here.

Everything in this book could be reduced to a sentence or even just a word or two. If you get this and understand it deeply, none of the rest of the book would be necessary. I want you to get this! Reflect on it deeply. What is this book, LIFE ON YOUR TERMS, really about? Think on this.

Stay in touch. See you in an online program or at a live event or the next book. Meanwhile, live life on your terms. Create your best life ever! Celebrate everything.

~ Rex

PS My online courses, live events, and workshops, provide you with powerful, tried and true principles and practices you can learn and take action on to make your life so much more wonderful. You'll find the programs life-transforming, easy to apply and fun too!

WHAT PEOPLE ARE SAYING

"I've spent over 30 years seeking out the top experts in human performance. There is nothing I've found that comes close to Mind Design. It is the ultimate life enhancement experience!" — Michael Halbfish, Lawyer, Bethlehem PA

"Mind Design is a game changer! It is the missing link between LOA, NLP, Hypnosis, Meditation, EFT & DHE. The support and feedback in the training is like nothing I've ever experienced before in 14 years of formal practice and 26 years of personal practice. You owe it to yourself and those you care about to look into this training!!" — Tim Shay, Musician, Philadelphia, PA

"My life changed the day I first met you which is quite funny as I was in the middle of Tony Robbins year-long Mastery University but nothing I found there ever compared to what I discovered with you, and now, all these years later, Mind Design! You truly are the gift that goes on giving, Rex." — Kathy Strong, NLP Trainer, Coach, Bleadon, England

"Mind Design helps me choose amazing thinking instead of habitual thoughts that aren't useful. I form new habits in thought and feeling that result in actions that get me my goals. The possibilities are endless." — Robert Bogsten, Copyrighter, Turku, Finland

"I can create instant magic effortlessly regardless of circumstances. In short, Mind Design helps me discover that I can be an excellent Magician with consistent Mind Design practice." — Ponsi Swett, CNHP and Wellness Consultant, Dayton OH

"I am so grateful to have found you on my journey Rex Sikes you are doing amazing things for this world." — Brian Alexander, Cross Fit Owner Entrepreneur, Chicago IL

"I really appreciate the empowering questions. Few days ago I was feeling a little blasé about things and then I started using the questions and immediately & incredibly it put me in a positive powerful resourceful state and still continues. Thank you Rex" — Richard Duggal, Speaker, Trainer, Toronto, CA

"Rex is one of the very best listeners I have ever had the pleasure of meeting. He cares about you, your striving, your challenges, your concerns. Rex is one of the most profoundly powerful communicators, yet he never towers over you on a stage. He walks his talk, and talks his walk, but WITH you in the trenches. As a professional networker with some 35,000 people in my organization, I'm primarily a trainer and I have modeled many excellent trainers, from Richard Bandler, to Anthony Robbins, Zig Zigler, Jim Rohn, just to mention a few, and to say that Rex towers above them all would be beside the point because he doesn't need the platform, the lights, the position, and ego. Rex holds his own against anyone I have ever heard and seen, primarily because he really cares about his students!" — Dan Anderson, Diamond Executive, MLM Co. Bruxelles, Belgium

IDEA Seminars, Rex Sikes Educational Programs

For More Information Or To Order Visit
IDEA-seminars.com

You are always welcome to participate in Rex's live and online events to further your learning and skyrocket your abilities. Perhaps, you are interested in Rex coaching you. Contact IDEA Seminars to get more books or products for your company and to give as gifts.

- How To Use Your Imagination And Visualize — Get Tesla and Einstein
- Got Problems You Need To Get Over — Get Letting Go
- Develop A Powerful Attitude When You Need One — Get Attitude Activator™
- Want To Communicate Powerfully And Effectively To Help Others And Yourself — Get How To Get People To Do What You Want™ & B.A.N.K.Code.
- Want Techniques For Your Personal Transformation And To Help Others — Get The Ultimate NLP Home Study Course™
- Skyrocket You Manifesting Power And Abundance — Get Change Your Thoughts And Transform Your Life
- Want To Create Your Best Life Ever — Get Mind Design™
- Read Rex's book — Life On Your Terms

To order programs and products and to get information on live events and seminars use the link below.

For More Information Or To Order Visit Idea-seminars.com

Thank You

Hidden within these pages: for you who have read this far I said in the beginning of this book, to maximize your learning and retention and to assist you in learning more easily and rapidly I use whole-brain, accelerated and peripheral-learning approaches. There are many ways to read it. You can read all the text, or you can go through and just read all the bold headlines. Do both at different times. You may have noticed topics, themes and phrases repeating. That is to help you wire it in. The more you repeat, the more you remember it. The better you get to know it. I've used the devices of underlining, bolding, capitalization, punctuation or the lack of it, and have used language in unconventional and colloquial ways to speak to both your conscious and non-conscious mind. I have repeated rhetorical questions for you to consider. Therefore, it may not read like a book you are used to reading, BUT it is more conversational and is how the brain processes. This is to get you to stop and re-read. It is designed to get you to slow down and think and reflect or consider what is being said and what is meant. It is me speaking to you. Coaching you. Everything is designed to get you to reflect, review, retain and recall.

ABOUT THE AUTHOR

Rex Steven Sikes, has four decades experience helping thousands of people transform their minds and lives. His innovations include Mind Design™ and Directed Questions™ and The Attitude Activator™. He conducts workshops and seminars live and online in Whole Brain and Accelerated Learning, the Law of Attraction (LOA), Mind Design™ and more. Sikes is founder of IDEA Seminars. Rex has appeared on numerous television and radio shows and can be found on youtube.